A
The Story of West Country C

Front cover: Black-eyed Sue and Sweet Poll of Plymouth, taking leave of their lovers, Cartoon, 1794. (By courtesy of the Mitchell Library, Sydney)

A sketch of convicts in Australia, c1800.

AUSTRALIA BOUND!

The Story of West Country Connections, 1688-1888

Martyn Brown

Foreword by H.R.H. The Duke of Kent
President of the Britain-Australia
Bicentennial Committee

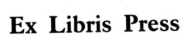

First published in 1988 by
Ex Libris Press
1 The Shambles
Bradford on Avon
Wiltshire

Typeset in 11 on 13 point Plantin by
Saxon Printing Ltd., Derby
Printed in Great Britain by A.Wheaton & Co. Ltd., Exeter

For Diana

ISBN 0 948578 08 4

Other books by Martyn Brown:
Somerset (Shire Publications, 1980)
A Somerset Camera (Dovecote Press, 1983)

CONTENTS

As President of the Britain-Australia Bicentennial Committee, I am pleased to contribute a Foreword to this new book by Martyn Brown.

There will be many books published during 1988 to commemorate the 200 years since the founding of the first settlement in Australia. What makes this book unique is that it focuses on the particular connections between the south-western counties of England and the newest continent. Mr. Brown is a professional historian who has long held an interest in rural economy and the significance of emigration in the shaping of his local landscape. But the book offers more than a monograph on the social and economic effects of a movement of population.

"Australia Bound!" attempts to recount the major contribution of people from the West of England to the founding of Australia. The author's starting point has been to examine the many evidences of Australian associations he has found, then to investigate and to trace where possible the antipodean fate of his many characters. The result is not only a representative sample of these associations but also an extremely readable account of the founding of a continent.

Of the convict settlements there is much, but
there is a good deal more besides, such as the story of
William Dampier, the sea-captain from Somerset, who in
1688 became the first Englishman to set foot on
Australian soil. There are some graphic accounts of
the voyage to Australia from the pens of various 'free
settlers' which encourage the reader to almost feel he
is there, with high hopes but little real knowledge of
what lay ahead, travelling steerage, in the last
century. There are sheep farmers from Somerset, miners
from Devon and Cornwall, fortune hunters galore during
the Gold Rush of the early 1850's and intrepid
explorers of that vast and inhospitable land.

To everyone with an interest in the early days of
Australia, and in the people who first left Britain to
start a new life there, I can strongly recommend this
absorbing and entertaining account.

H.R.H. The Duke of Kent
President
Britain-Australia Bicentennial
    Committee

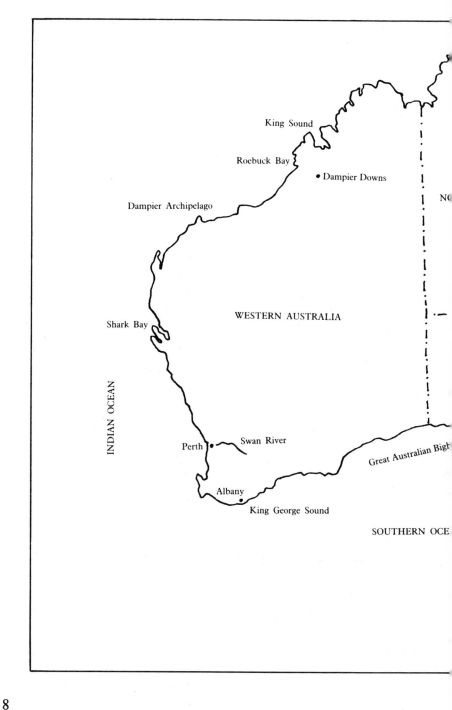

King Sound

Roebuck Bay

• Dampier Downs

Dampier Archipelago

N(

WESTERN AUSTRALIA

Shark Bay

INDIAN OCEAN

Perth • — Swan River

Great Australian Bigh

Albany
•
King George Sound

SOUTHERN OCE

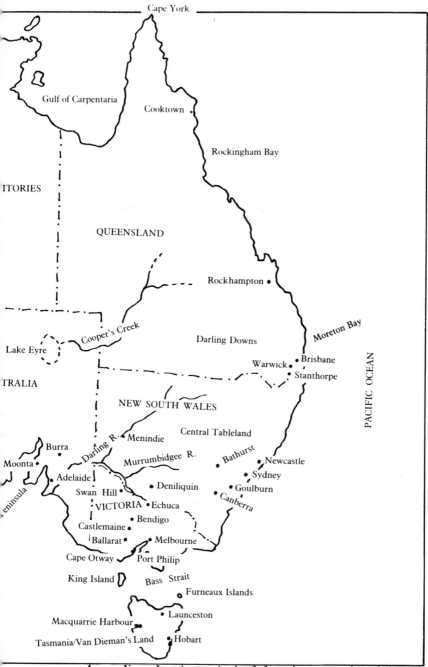

Cape York

Gulf of Carpentaria

Cooktown

Rockingham Bay

ITORIES

QUEENSLAND

Rockhampton

Cooper's Creek

Darling Downs

Moreton Bay

Lake Eyre

Warwick • Brisbane

TRALIA

Stanthorpe

PACIFIC OCEAN

NEW SOUTH WALES

Menindie

Central Tableland

Burra

Darling R.

Bathurst

Moonta •

Murrumbidgee R.

Newcastle

Adelaide

Sydney

Swan Hill

Deniliquin

Goulburn

eninsula

VICTORIA • Echuca

Canberra

Castlemaine •

Bendigo

Ballarat •

Melbourne

Cape Otway

Port Philip

King Island

Bass Strait

Furneaux Islands

Macquarrie Harbour

Launceston

Tasmania/Van Dieman's Land

Hobart

Australia, showing principal locations mentioned in the text

Ilfracombe

• Barnstaple

Appledore

Weare Giffard

• Hatherleig

• Launceston

Chagford

Moretonha

• St Agnes

Horrabridge

• Bodmin

Plymouth
Plympton

• Liskeard

Sou

Wembury

Redruth

• Truro

Fowey

Penzance

Germoe

Falmouth

Newlyn

• Breage

South-West England, showing the principal locations mentioned in the text

Acknowledgements:

By the very nature of a book of this sort, it is necessary to look towards all sorts of people for help; whether it be the librarians and archivists of the official establishments with relevant collections, or the chatty stranger who drops a vital clue to an intractable part of a story, or a family historian who has ploughed through miles of microfiche to trace a black-sheep relative – each contribution has played its part, and I am grateful to them all. Histories of this kind rely on connections, and I hope that by listing those who have helped me, others pursuing similar research in future or wishing to expand some of the themes touched within this book, will be able to retrace my footsteps without too much difficulty.

There are two people in Australia, whom I have never met, but who have inspired me with enthusiasm and helped unstintingly. First Carolyn Randle who has generously contributed time, energy and original research, and without whom the book would be much the poorer; and second Marjorie Butler, whose books, *Convict by Choice* and *Settler by Succession*, originally fired my interest; to them both, my special gratitude.

Otherwise, thanks are due to the following:

Richard Allen (Jersey, C.I.), Mark Baker (Pewsey, Wilts.), BBC Radio Devon, Ann Beeching (Britain-Australia Bicentennial Committee, London), Michael Billett (Frome, Somerset), J.D.Bisdee OBE (Midhurst, West Sussex), Dr Steven Blake (Cheltenham Art Gallery and Museums), Dr M.Brayshay (Plymouth, Devon), David Bromwich (Local History Library, Taunton), Mrs Brownjohn (Limington, Hants), Nigel Buckler (West Country Tourist Board, Exeter), Mrs J.Marjorie Butler (Mt. Eliza, Victoria) (AUSTIN family), Mrs P.Carew Hunt (Westbury, Wilts), Major J.Carroll (Dorset Military Museum, Dorchester), Jonathan Carter (Jersey, C.I.), Michael Champion, Dr J.Chandler (Wiltshire Local Studies Library, Trowbridge), Mrs A.J.Colquitt-Craven (Wadebridge, Cornwall), Miss Pat Cotton (West Bradley, Somerset) (AUSTIN, NORRIS), Mr Michael Cowen (Salisbury, Wilts.), Mrs E.J.Drew (Plymouth, Devon) (BARTLETT), Colin and Joan Duplock (Cairns, Queensland), Miss Q.Dyer (Teignmouth, Devon) (DYER), Miss Jane Evans (Woodspring Museum, Weston-super-Mare) (TABART), Mrs M.Fletcher (Donhead St.Andrew, Dorset), Carol Fosset (Cooktown, Queensland), Peter and Loraine Fox (Canberra, ACT), Richard Glynn esq (South Zeal, Okehampton, Devon), Dr A.Grant (Devon), J.Griffiths (Cirencester, Gloucestershire), Mary Gryspeerdt (Somerset Rural Life Museum, Glastonbury, Somerset), C.H.Hallett esq (Cannington, Somerset), Pam Hodgman (Brisbane, Queensland)(TABART), Mrs Joyce Jenkins (Tisbury, Wilts.), Roger Jones (my publisher), W.Allan Jones (Launceston, Tasmania) (MUDGE, CHAMPION), Mrs N.Lavery (Brisbane, Queensland) (BROWNJOHN), Mrs M.Leneham (Lane Cove, New South Wales), Local History Library (Plymouth, Devon), Steven Locke (S.W.Area Museum Council), Mrs F.Mapstone (Glastonbury, Somerset), Dr C.Marshall (Exeter, Devon) (ROWE), Marjorie McElhone (Southport, Queensland), Mr McLennan (Exeter, Devon) (HICKS), Mrs M.Mimmack (Jersey, C.I.), Mrs Pauline Morgan (Picnic Point, New South Wales) (HOWE), Mrs Bettie Morris (Wylye, Wilts.) (POPJAY), National Maritime Museum (Greenwich, London), Michael Oxenbould (Newton Abbot, Devon), Bob and Jacqueline Patter (Crediton, Devon), Richard de Peyer (S.W.Area Museum Council), Mrs Carolyn Randle (Ascott, Queensland), Mr Ridgeway (Dulverton, Somerset), Lady St Aubyn (Pencarrow, Cornwall), W.Scutt (Plymouth Museum and Art Gallery), Mr and Mrs M.Sheppard (Newbury, Berks), David and Caroline Simington (Bath, Avon), Mrs Connie Smith (Bath, Avon), Mr and Mrs J.Somers Cocks (Newton Abbot, Devon), Somerset County Record Office (Taunton), Miss M.Syvret(Société Jersiaise), John Tabart and Anthony Tabart (Victoria), Ken Tabart (Launceston, Tasmania), Mrs Kathy Tanner (Cookworthy Museum, Kingsbridge, Devon), Mrs Elaine Thomson (Pomona, Queensland) (COX, ORANGE), Mrs H.Tomlin (Southampton, Hants), John Vivian esq (Chudleigh, Devon), West Country Studies Library (Exeter, Devon), Wiltshire County Record Office (Trowbridge).

I would also like to thank my wife, Jane, whose patience survived the long Summer holidays and enabled me to complete the text approximately on time.

INTRODUCTION

A glimpse at an atlas map of Tasmania reveals a tantalising mass of place-names clearly derived from the English West Country – Launceston, Devonport, Bridport, Tamar, Portland, Cornwall – what are they doing there, 15,000 miles away on the wrong side of the globe? Similarly, a handful of enquiries in any West Country town will quickly establish a host of local connections with Australia of one sort or another; what led to these links and associations? Why so many? And why so strong? At least four out of every ten households in Britain have direct connections with Australia today, and despite immigration from many other parts of the world, the majority of Australians are of British descent. This book tries to unravel some of these West Country connections.

I have never attempted nor been interested (so far) to trace my own family's links and the book is no genealogical report; rather it attempts to describe a sample of these regional associations – from starting points as various as the Red Signpost near Bloxworth (Dorset) to the model of the fishing lugger *Mystery* in the Cornwall County Museum, from the Australian flag fluttering in Wembury (Devon) parish church to an inscribed stone near Tilshead (Wiltshire) on the edge of Salisbury Plain – the legends and history behind each of these memorials have been the subject of my research. Naturally it has proved an impossible task; like pebbles on the beach, for every stone turned, thousands of others remain firmly face down. In that respect it is a frustrating and never-ending race; far more has had to be left out than could possibly be included, and the selection of what to include is necessarily arbitrary. Some stones have been turned to reveal such a mass of information that their mention here may, I hope, encourage others to delve more deeply. I am painfully conscious of numerous omissions and no doubt will become aware of many more as soon as the type is set.

Deliberately, much of the text consists of quotations drawn from journals, diaries, letters and contemporary publications; they give a fragment of insight into the perceptions of their authors, one hundred, two hundred and three hundred years ago. From these extracts we can attempt to get into the minds of the early explorers, the transported convicts and the adventurous settlers to try and understand how they viewed this new and unknown land, their feelings at leaving loved ones behind, and their brave or fearful anticipation of the future. Their words are far more vivid and telling, and of course are uncoloured by the trappings of the 20th century.

Unfortunately only a small fraction of my research has been of primary sources; I have had to rely on the work of others, notably genealogists; but whenever and wherever possible I have followed trails to local record offices, newspapers, churchyards and, above all, to private individuals who invariably have provided the flesh with which to embellish the bones of statistics and official records.

The spur to this publication has been the activity of the Britain-Australia Bicentennial Committee celebrating the anniversary of the first permanent European settlement in Australia in 1788; it is therefore with some pride that the first chapter of this book establishes the West Country's claim to celebrate an older anniversary: the tercentenary of the first Englishman to set foot on Australian soil in 1688 – William Dampier of East Coker, near Yeovil.

Martyn Brown
Exeter, September 1987

1   FIRST FOOTFALL

On the north wall of the nave of St Michael's Church, East Coker, a pretty Ham stone village three miles south west of Yeovil, there is a sparkling brass memorial; it is to one William Dampier, born in the parish, at Hymerford House, in 1651. The story of West Country links with Australia begins here, because it was from this Somerset village that William Dampier set out as a young man to become the first Englishman to set foot on a white sandy beach, 13,000 miles away – in Australia.

It is an odd coincidence that Dampier's first footfall on the north west shore of New Holland, as Australia was then called, preceeded the first permanent European settlement by exactly 100 years; and if that is odd, it is even more so to contemplate the fact that it took so long for explorers, voyagers and sailors to delineate, or even to be sure of the existence of the largest island in the world.

Australian aboriginals had of course spread throughout the continent from about 30,000 BC; they had hopped, skipped and paddled from Asia, down the chain of islands forming modern Indonesia, at a time when the sea level was significantly lower than it is today. The straits between Timor and Melville Island, and New Guinea and Cape York would have been narrower, perhaps even narrow enough for a glimpse of a distant shore – on a clear day – enough to encourage an adventurous boatman. Some 15,000 years ago, as the ice sheets began to melt as a result of a gradual rise in temperatures throughout the world, the land mass of Australia became isolated – until about 5,000 years ago when the present coastline was established.

That coast of Australia had been charted from the early seventeenth century by Dutch traders heading for Java. They rounded Cape Horn and were swept speedily eastwards by the Roaring Forties; their unfortunate problem was that, in that age, the chronometer was unknown and it was virtually impossible for a navigator at sea to determine his longitude with any accuracy. Sailors were left to guess when they had gone far enough and should turn north. Some ships strayed too far south and east and when they changed course, they found their way blocked by the inhospitable towering cliffs of the Great Australian Bight. In 1627 a Dutch ship sailed 1,000 miles along this southern coast of Australia and was only 500 sea miles from the site of modern Adelaide before she retreated.[1] Other ships, following a lesser latitude, just ran into Australia's west coast, somewhat unexpectedly; some managed to zig-zag their way north, not easy on a 1,000 mile long windward coast, others were lost.

By 1650, two-thirds of the Australian coastline had been traced, much of it by that talented seafarer Abel Tasman – but Australia appeared to offer very little of substance to these Dutch traders; the natives had no marketable goods, the coastal lands grew nothing that was of any value in Europe, and there was no easy access inland to encourage prospectors for minerals.

Throughout the seventeenth century, the details of the position and extent of a Great Southern Continent, *Terra Australis Incognita*, were the subject of much speculation; a translation of Tasman's journal describing his discovery of Tasmania (Van Dieman's Land) was not published in London until 1694. Dampier's assumption, on all his wanderings, was that existing maps of the Pacific were 'all false'[2] – but with few technical advantages over his predecessors in the sixteenth century, it is hardly surprising that the accuracy of his own bearings was no better.

William Dampier was baptised on 5 September, 1651, the second son of George and Ann; his father was a substantial tenant farmer; their house, one of the principal properties of the local Squire – Colonel Helyar – an imposing medieval building with a two-storey porch and adjacent farm buildings. William was sent to school possibly in Yeovil, or to the Grammar School in Crewkerne. He recorded, several years later, in his Journal, that:[3]

> My friends did not originally design me for the sea, but bred me at school till I came to years fit for a trade. But upon the death of my father and mother [his mother died, a widow, in 1665], they who had the disposal of me took other measures; and having remov'd me from the Latine School to learn Writing and Arithmetick, they soon after placed me with a Master of a Ship at Weymouth, complying with the inclinations I had very early of seeing the World.

With the Weymouth skipper he made a short voyage to France and returned with his appetite whetted for adventure; almost immediately, he set off again, this time to Newfoundland. Perhaps he was not quite as tough as might be imagined because he described that he was so horribly 'pinched' by the rigour of that cold climate that he swore he would never sail so far north again.[4]

William returned to East Coker where, no doubt, he stayed with his elder brother, George; but he could not settle to country life and kept darting off to London trying to get an offer of a 'warm voyage'. Eventually he succeeded and was employed as an able seaman 'before the mast' on the East Indiaman, the *John and Martha*, of London, under

Hymerford House, East Coker, near Yeovil, Somerset; William Dampier's birthplace.

Captain Earning, bound for the Dutch Spice Islands; they sailed to Bantam, Java – William using any opportunity on board to study the practise of navigation. After a little over a year at sea, they returned to Plymouth.

The King of England had, almost at that moment, declared war on Holland, for the second time within a few years, and William, still thirsting for excitement, enlisted on the King's ship, *Royal Prince*, under the command of Sir Edward Spragge – a somewhat foolhardy captain with a reputation for reckless courage. Most of the rest of the crew were undoubtedly 'pressed' men and not at all keen on the promise of action ahead. As luck would have it, William fell sick and was 'put on board a hospital ship' and missed the ensuing engagement – the Battle of Texel.

About this time, George Dampier moved from East Coker to a neighbouring estate – 'Porton, near Breadport, Dorset' – as it was described in William's will. William went there to convalesce but did not stay long and 'with my health I recovered my old inclination for the Sea'.[5] His father's old landlord, Colonel Helyar, had interests in the West Indies – indeed, he had imported negro servants to East Coker and one 'black-a-moor' was baptised in the Parish Church in the year of William's birth – and William was made 'a reasonable offer' to go out and manage one of the Colonel's plantations in Jamaica. In March or April 1674, William set sail, working his passage on the *Content*, with Captain Kent.

After 6 months on the plantation, followed by odd-jobbing about the Caribbean – notably as a logwood-cutter in the swamps of the Yucatan, enduring storms, mosquitos and Spaniards, he hit his beam-end and 'was forced' so he says 'to range about to seek a subsistence in company with some privateers then in the Bay';[6] so began his career as a pirate.

William returned to England in 1678, hastily married a girl called Judith, and was off again the following year to rejoin the buccaneers. He had begun his famous Journal, not to record his private life, but to note assiduously his observations, and hydrographical details which were to make his *Discourse*[7] a model recommended by Admiral Nelson to his midshipmen 100 years later. He protected his book through an incredible series of watery disasters – on one occasion stuffing it inside a bamboo pole, then sealing up the ends, and using the pole as a float to cross a raging torrent.[8] There is no doubt that amongst his buccaneering friends he was regarded as the acknowledged, if unofficial, expert on all

Portrait of William Dampier by Thomas Murray, c1698. The portrait was ordered by the distinguished collector, Sir Hans Sloane. (By courtesy of the National Portrait Gallery, London).
S.T.Coleridge commented on the picture: 'Look at the face of old Dampier, a rough sailor, but a man of exquisite mind. How soft is the air of his countenance, how delicate the shape of his temples'. (Table Talk of Samuel Taylor Coleridge, *London, 1884, p.145.*)

matters to do with navigation – and all this learnt from practical experience snatched between duties.

In 1686, at the age of 35, William Dampier was appointed pilot, or navigating officer, on the privateer *Cygnet* under Captain Swan; they loped about the Caribbean for a time, then Dampier and Swan, whom Wilkinson described as 'simply a fat humbug',[9] hatched a plan to cross the Pacific. They hugged the coast of South America down to Cape Horn and sailed up the west coast to the Galapagos Islands and Mexico; having nonchalantly raided a couple of small towns, they finally set off on 31 March and were treated to 'a fresh Trade Wind'.

The crew was a motley bunch and troublesome from the start, insisting on an increase in rations; they made Guam with just three days' food left. William afterwards discovered that had the food run out, the men planned 'first to kill Captain Swan and eat him.... and after him all of us who were accessory in promoting the undertaking this Voyage'. They roved the Philippines, then abandoned their Captain on Mindanao, the southernmost of that group of islands. The command of *Cygnet* was taken over by one of the other pirates, John Read, who came from Bristol. Quite unexpectedly on 27 December 1687, they suddenly decided to take a look at '*Terra Australis Incognita*', just 'to see what that country would afford us'.[10]

It seems odd that William did not make more of this exploration in his Journal; he noted casually that 'it is not yet determined whether it [Australia or New Holland as it was called on contemporary maps] is an Island or a Main Continent' adding that he is convinced that 'it joins neither to Asia, Africa nor America'. Their voyage was uneventful and on 14 January 1688, they made their landfall in the latitude of 16° 50'; there are many theories as to precisely where this was – King Sound on the north west coast is one possibility.

William and his colleagues camped on the beach; they made contact with the aborigines whom he described as:

> the miserablest people in the World. The Hodmadods [Hottentots] of Monomatapa, though a nasty People, yet for Wealth are Gentlemen to these...and setting aside their humane shape, they differ little from Brutes. They are tall, strait-bodied, and thin, with small long limbs. They have great Heads, round Foreheads, and great Brows. Their Eye-lids are always half closed, to keep the Flies out of their Eyes....therefore they cannot see far....They are

long visaged, and of very unpleasing aspect, having no one graceful feature in their faces.

They have no houses, but lye in the open Air, without any covering, the earth being their bed, and the Heaven their canopy.... The Earth affords them no food at all. There is neither Herb, Pulse, nor any sort of Grain, for them to eat, that we saw; nor any sort of Bird or Beast that they can catch, having no instruments wherewithal to do so.

I did not perceive that they did worship anything.[11]

Such views, though bigoted and ignorant, were typical of the early explorers and what is worse, they appear to have influenced the attitudes of many the first settlers in the late eighteenth and nineteenth centuries to such an extent that aborigines were hunted and killed like animals and in Tasmania their race was totally wiped out. One particular feature of these people that was found hard to explain was their lack of interest in things European – William Dampier noticed this when a couple of aborigines were taken on board their vessel to be given a meal: 'they merely gobbled up any food within reach, without lifting their eyes from it, or displaying the faintest interest in their strange surroundings'[12] and in the following century, and 2,000 miles away on the other side of the continent both Captain Cook and Admiral Phillip recorded the same characteristic.

The *Cygnet* left Australia at the beginning of March, and after a saga of adventures that would fill a *Boy's Own* Annual William returned to England in 1691, having circumnavigated the world. His souvenir of the trip was a tatooed native chief, called Jeoly, from Mindanao, in whom he had a half share and planned to recoup his investment by displaying the poor man around the country. A London broadsheet announced:

> his whole body is curiously and most exquisitely painted and stained full of variety of invention, with prodigeous Art and Skill perform'd....he is exposed to publick view every day from the 16th day of this instant June, at his lodgings at the Blew Boar's Head in Fleet Street, near Water Lane.

Short of ready cash, William sold his share, but Jeoly was hoicked about England until he died of smallpox in Oxford.

The publication of his Journal launched William into the public eye; he was taken up by the President of the Royal Society, Charles

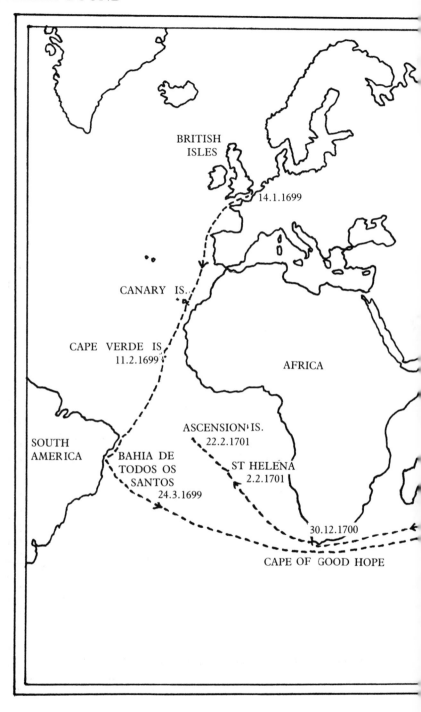

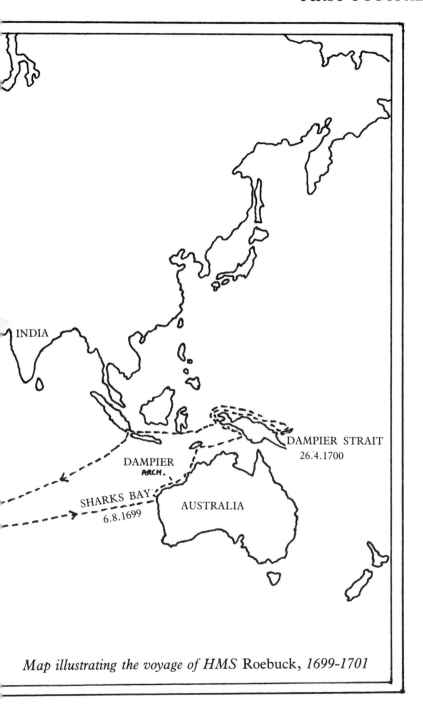

Map illustrating the voyage of HMS Roebuck, *1699-1701*

Montague, to whom he had dedicated the volume and, amongst others, he met Sir Hans Sloane who ordered his portrait by Thomas Murray. He was invited to dine by Samuel Pepys, and his fellow guest happened to be that other diarist John Evelyn:

> *6 August.* I dined with Mr.Pepys, where was Capt. Dampier, who had become a famous Buccaneer, had brought hither the painted Prince Job [Jeoly], and printed a relation of his strange adventure, and his observations. He is now going abroad again by the King's encouragement, who furnished a ship of 290 tons. He seemed a more modest man than one would imagine by the relation of the crew he had assorted with. He brought a map of his observations of the course of the Winds in the South Sea, and assured us that the maps hitherto extant were all false as to the Pacific Sea, which he makes on the South of the Line, that on the North and running by the coast of Peru being extremely tempestuous.[13]

The new voyage, refered to by Evelyn, was to be in HMS *Roebuck*, and William, sponsored by the Crown, was commissioned to explore the coasts of Australia and New Guinea, to discover, once and for all, the precise extent of these far off lands. William clearly understood the important opportunity this offered; amongst other things he considered, prophetically, that Australia was 'a country likely to contain gold'.

The usual saga of delays that seems to have bogged every voyage of this kind postponed their departure. Whilst the stores were being stowed aboard, William was already quarrelling with his second-in-command, Lieutenant Fisher, a regular officer of the King's Navy, who took a dim view of his commanding officer's previous career. The *Roebuck* carried 12 guns, a crew of 50 men and boys and was provisioned for 20 months. At last they set sail from the Downs on 14 January 1699.

The problems with Fisher continued with the voyage under way, and culminated in William turning him off the boat in Bahia de Todos os Santos, Brazil, and depositing him in gaol. Meanwhile William and the rest of the crew enjoyed a month's stay, exploring the country and stocking up with oranges, rum and sugar. On 23 April the *Roebuck* weighed anchor and put to sea; Fisher was abandoned, to be returned to England later by the Portuguese Governor.

They passed the Cape on 6 June, and their next sight of land was the coast of Australia; Hughes, the master, recorded on 31 July that he could see land which 'promises very barren....neither trees nor bushes'. They nosed cautiously into a bay, the ship's boat going ahead sounding with the lead. William christened it 'Shark's Bay', on account of the great number of sharks they saw in the water. They landed to search, in vain, for fresh water to replenish the barrels on board; supplies were low and the crew were getting restless.

William decided to follow the coast northwards; they carefully navigated through a group of islands, now called the Dampier Archipelago, still searching for water. They landed again on the mainland, at a spot still known as Roebuck Bay; about 50 miles inland a small settlement, Dampier Downs, is shown on modern maps. A bunch of aborigines turned up who appeared hostile; William tried to alleviate the situation, but seeing one of his young sailors wounded in the face by a wooden lance, he shot one of the aborigines and the rest drew back. Although he regretted his action, he again noted that the Australian aborigines 'have the most unpleasant looks and the worst features of any people that I saw'.

They found 'a little brackish water', but the men were 'growing scorbutic' for lack of water and fresh food, and were becoming increasingly irascible. 'If it were not', said William, 'for that sort of pleasure which results from the Discovery even of the barrenest spot upon the Globe, this coast of New Holland would not have charmed me much'.[14] With that, he left Australia and set his course for the island of Timor.

They explored the coast of New Guinea, discovering and naming the strait which divides New Britain from New Guinea – Dampier Strait; then set off for home. At Ascension Island the *Roebuck* sprang a leak, in fact she was leaking like a sieve – they abandoned her near the shore, having made a raft to carry the crew's chests and bedding to the beach. William and his men survived for five weeks, a Robinson Crusoe existence, on the uninhabited island, living on turtles, until three men-o-war and an East Indiaman came in to shelter and they were rescued.

So the great voyage of discovery ended; William had not succeeded in answering any of the outstanding questions about Australia. Back in England he faced a court-martial; not so much for losing his vessel, which could be satisfactorily explained, but for dumping an officer of the Royal Navy into a grubby Portuguese gaol and leaving him there – that was another matter altogether; and Fisher had had plenty of time to brood over his fate and to prepare his case thoroughly.

The President of the court-martial, Sir Cloudesley Shovell, concluded that:

> Captain William Dampier has been guilty of very Hard and Cruel Usage towards Lieutenant Fisher, in beating him aboard ye sd. ship, and confining him in Irons a considerable time, and afterwards imprisoning him on shore in a strange country...and itt is farther the opinion of ye Court that the said Captain Dampier is not a fitt person to be employ'd as Commandr. of any of Her Majesty's ships.[15]

The verdict apparently caused William little harm; only ten months later the London Gazette reported that:

> Captain William Dampier, being prepared to depart on another voyage to the West Indies, had the honour to kiss Her Majesty's hand, being introduced by His Royal Highness, the Lord High Admiral [Prince George of Denmark].[16]

Back in East Coker, the memorial to William Dampier is embossed with his portrait and with that of the sort of ship he sailed; the inscription reads:

WILLIAM DAMPIER
Buccaneer, Explorer, Hydrographer.
Thrice he circumnavigated the Globe and, first of all Englishmen, explored and described the coast of Australia.
An exact observer of all things in Earth, Sea and Air, he recorded the knowledge won by years of danger and hardship in Books of Voyages and a Discourse on Winds, Tides and Currents which Nelson bade his midshipmen to study and Humboldt praised for scientific worth.
Born at East Coker 1651
He died in London 1715
and lies buried in an unknown grave.

The world is apt to judge of everything by the success, and whosoever has ill fortune will hardly be allowed a good name.

William Dampier's memorial in St. Michael's Church, East Coker.

2 ENDEAVOUR AND RESOLUTION

Throughout the eighteenth century questions about the possible existence of a Great Southern Continent continued, despite the distractions of the Seven Years' War, the American War of Independance and growing social tensions at home. Swift's account of *Gulliver's Travels* and the publication of journals of other more down to earth voyages helped to kindle the interest, while the bubble-burst of the notorious South Sea Company drew attention to the hazards of commercial speculation in the Pacific.

The big problem for explorers and navigators was their reliance on the wind; rounding Cape Horn, the prevailing westerlies and drifting icebergs tended to deflect ships to the north or north-west. Even when Captain Samuel Wallis, a Cornishman, and Tobias Furneaux, from Swilly, now part of Plymouth, were sent in the *Dolphin* from England in 1766 with specific instructions to sail due west from the Horn in search of the 'missing' continent, they were unable to fight their way against the westerlies in high latitudes. They veered north west to warmer seas, and in latitude 17° south, found Tahiti instead.[1] Wallis and Furneaux returned to England in May 1768, just in time to pass on the news of this pleasant island and handy base in mid-ocean to James Cook.

Philip Carteret, from Jersey, in the *Swallow*, a 'rotten little ship', had not been able to keep up with Wallis; but he made a brave voyage to Pitcairn Island, the Society Islands, the Santa Cruz islands, four of which he named Jersey, Guernsey, Alderney and Sark, and the Solomon's; he discovered the narrow strait between New Britain and New Ireland, St George's Channel; but sailed too far north to catch sight of the Australian coast.[2]

On 26 August 1768, Captain James Cook sailed from Plymouth, in the *Endeavor*, a converted Whitby collier, on a scientific expedition to observe the transit of Venus from the clear skies of the Pacific; the new-found island of Tahiti was to be his destination. He also carried secret instructions from the Admiralty: since 'there is reason to imagine that a continent, or land of great extent, may be found to the southward of the track...of former navigators', he was to sail to the latitude of 40° south in search of it and, if successful, to explore the coast, and the nature of the people, of the soil and of its products.

Cook spent six months poking about the coasts of New Zealand and reaching the conclusion that it formed no part of the great southern continent, then he continued westwards. On 19 April 1770 the east coast of Australia was sighted and ten days later they landed at Stingray Bay. The botanists on board, led by Joseph Banks and Daniel Solander, could not believe their eyes; the welcoming shore was ablaze with flowering shrubs unknown to European science. For a week they gorged on study and renamed the bay Botany Bay.

Early explorers were amazed at the unique flora and fauna of Australia; hence the name Botany Bay; a kangaroo.

Cook's reaction to the natives was markedly different from Dampier's:

> They may appear to some to be the most wretched people on earth, but in reality they are far happier than we Europeans; being wholly unacquainted not only with the superfluous but the necessary Conveniences so much sought after in Europe, they are happy in not knowing the use of them. They live in Tranquility which is not disturb'd by the Inequality of Condition.[3]

Leaving Botany Bay, they followed the coast northwards; it is said that whilst Captain Cook was munching his breakfast, the look-out at the masthead, a man named Jackson, spotted the entrance to what appeared to be a good harbour; and the Captain, half in derision, named it Port Jackson – little realising the future of that great bay at the head of which the city of Sydney was to be built.

Edging further north, Cook and the *Endeavor* became entrapped between the Great Barrier Reef and the eastern coastline stretching 2,000 miles towards Cape York; the ship struck the reef and limped into the mouth of a sandy river to seek shelter and a temporary home, where repairs could be completed. This first European settlement in Australia lasted only 48 days. The ship was beached on the south bank of the river which the crew named the Endeavor; stores were unloaded, tents pitched and a blacksmith's forge set up – on the site of the settlement now known as Cooktown, Queensland.[4] It was here that one of the ship's officers shot an animal later described as 'the typical animal of the country', called by the natives the 'kangaroo' or 'kangura'.

With the *Endeavor* sea-worthy once again, Cook pressed on; at Cape York he claimed possession of the whole of the east coast by the name of New South Wales, for his majesty King George III.

After three years at sea, Cook returned to England; he confided to a friend: 'I have made no great discoveries, yet I have explored more of the South Sea than all that have gone before me'. Perhaps one of Captain Cook's greatest contributions was his success at combatting scurvy – the scourge of long voyages; throughout the three-year voyage, not a man was lost through scurvy thanks to his regular issue of proper antiscorbutics – sauerkraut, malt and vinegar – as Robert Hughes so neatly concluded: 'Malt juice and pickled cabbage put Europeans in Australia, as microchip circuitry would put Americans on the moon'.[5]

One crewman of the *Endeavor* who was grateful to be returned safely to his West Country home in the village of Bishops Cannings in the Vale of Pewsey, Wiltshire, was William Bayley; he presented the organ to the parish church.[6]

No sooner was he back, than Cook was pressing for another chance to search some more for this elusive continent; at last on 23 June 1772 the Admiralty gave him his commission, and at the same time, appointed as his second-in-command Tobias Furneaux. They sailed from Plymouth Sound in the *Resolution* and the *Adventure* respectively on 13 July. They spent weeks dodging icebergs and riding out the 'roaring fifties' and finally Cook was able to conclude that there was not the least possibility of there being another southern continent unless very near the Pole.[7]

One consolation was Furneaux's landing on Tasmania, on 9 March 1773, to become the first Englishman to do so; he named the spot Adventure Bay, after his ship.[8] Furneaux sailed north along the east coast and then a short distance into Bass Strait – there was much speculation aboard the *Adventure* as to whether Tasmania was an island or not. Most of the officers and seamen were of the opinion that a strait existed north of Tasmania, but Furneaux was not convinced and when he was once again reunited with the *Resolution* in New Zealand, he reported to Captain Cook that Tasmania was part of the Australian mainland and only partly separated from it by a deep bay.[9]

Back home, the Government was struggling with one particularly intractable problem brought about by the war with America – ever since 1597, when an Act of Parliament was passed to authorize the 'banishment' of certain classes of criminals, prisoners had been transported, first to the West Indies and later to America. Quite naturally, following her independance, America refused to act as this dustbin for undesirables any longer. The prisons throughout Britain filled to overflowing; and as an emergency measure various disused naval vessels, or hulks, moored in the Thames, were fitted out as temporary gaols.

English criminal law in the late eighteenth century was in an unbelievable state. The policing system was primitive leaving the detection of criminals almost entirely to the activities of an unpaid magistracy or private societies for the prevention of crime. Though partially effective in rural areas, where the small population was well known, it was ludicrously inefficient in the growing cities. The only method of checking crime that Parliament could devise was that of prescribing heavier and heavier penalties to deter offenders – something in the region of 200 crimes were punishable by death, including stealing goods of the value of 40 shillings or more from a dwelling house, picking pockets of more than one shilling or stealing a sheep. Public executions were popular as spectacles of entertainment, attracting crowds as large as those for a modern Cup Final, followed up by broadsheets describing the scene in grimy and graphic detail; the hanging of brothers William and James Lightfoot, for example, in front of the gaol at Bodmin (Cornwall) in 1840 was watched by an estimated 20-25,000 people and 'the town of Bodmin.... presented the appearance of a fair'.[10] Mercifully many of those sentenced to execution were reprieved, on condition of their being transported to the colonies. Still more crimes were punishable by transportation in the first place and others by long prison sentences, some with hard labour and a public whipping thrown in.

Very soon, both the prisons and the hulks were overcrowded; the situation was becoming desperate. In 1779 a House of Commons committee was set up to determine where those sentenced to transportation could be sent; amongst others, Joseph Banks was invited to make recommendations and he enthused over the suitability of Botany Bay: the natives were cowardly, the weather was mild, the soil sufficient to

A public hanging; the frontispiece to Samuel Hook's The Life and Death of John Carpenter, *London, 1805.*

The prison hulk York *at Portsmouth; as many as 600 men and boys were jammed in as prison overspill, to await their transport to Australia.*

support a large number of people, there were no beasts of prey, but plenty of fish.[11] The committee deliberated – Gibralter was considered, and the west coast of Africa.

Meanwhile the problem increased; at Plymouth, the *Dunkirk* Hulk, a King's Ship, 'was appointed for the Reception of Prisoners from the Western Gaols'.[12] A report on the conditions on board the hulks in 1776 described 'sickly men....biscuits given out mouldy and green on both sides – no bedding, lay upon boards – bad smell'.[13] As many as 800 prisoners were confined on each ship, living in groups or wards of 20 or 30; during the day they were set to labour in the dockyards, but at night they were crammed in to the fetid vessel where 'the evil consequences of such associations may be easily conceived'.[14]

Prison reformers like Jeremy Bentham and John Howard canvassed for new-style penitentiaries where solitary confinement, instruction and well-regulated labour might rehabilitate – but sceptics doubted that this was possible and argued the existence of a 'criminal class', the pits of society who could, it was theorized, even be identified by their phrenology. The only solution was to rid civilisation of these people by physically removing them as far away as possible, 'beyond the seas'.

Transportation was a particularly harsh punishment, second in severity only to the death penalty. Far more than geographical removal and isolation, transportation was an emotional and psychological assault both on the criminal, who might have deserved it, and on his family – who almost certainly did not. Even a seven year sentence, to an unknown land beyond the frontiers of civilisation, seemed an impossibility to endure. With no news of a husband for years on end, what could the wife left to fend for herself and the children do?

Poor Law Settlement papers give some harrowing and very personal accounts of families, bereft in this way, as part of pleas for residency in a particular parish and rights to receive poor relief; in 1818, Sarah Dinham, for example, from Curry Rivel in Somerset gave evidence before Vincent Stuckey JP that:

> about 26 years ago she was married to John Dinham of Buckland St. Mary after which her husband lived with her for several years in the parish of Curry Rivell (sic) .....her husband was transported on a charge of sheepstealing... she hath never since heard from or of her said husband... that afterwards she resided in Buckland St. Mary for ten years or thereabouts with four of her children [Sarah, Thomas, Betty and Aaron], in the parish house...[15]

Similarly, Mary Hipsley, of Yatton (now Avon), who married one Joseph Willmott in about 1820, reported on oath that:

> After we had been married about five or six years the said Joseph Willmott was convicted of felony and sentenced to transportation for the term of his life. The said Joseph Willmott was transported accordingly to New South Wales and I heard from him shortly after his arrival there. It was within two years after his conviction that I so heard from him. On the sixth day of February in the year 1830 and not having heard of the said Joseph Willmott for more than seven years I married Charles Moore of Yatton aforesaid by whom I have since had two children namely Mary now aged two years and Martha aged about six months both of whom are now

living with me. Since I so married the said Charles Moore I have heard of my said husband Joseph Willmott and that he was alive so late as the 31st day of December 1830.....after he was transported and whilst I was living in the said parish of Yatton I received relief for several years from the Overseers of the poor...[16]

At the end of the eighteenth century there was little sensitivity to such hardships; Lord Beauchamp's committee reported that the rising tide of crime was 'in great Measure attributed to the Want of a proper place for the Transportation of Criminals'.[17] In addition to the eradication of the criminal class at home, convict labour in the colonies was both valuable and remedial. Beauchamp's committee voted for Das Voltas Bay, at the mouth of the Orange River in south-west Africa, as the ideal spot for this open gaol overseas – but a survey ship returned to describe sterile and dry soils, incapable of supporting any permanent settlement.

One Devon Member of Parliament, John Rolle, clearly concerned by the prison conditions in his constituency, corresponded with the Prime Minister, William Pitt, on the subject in June 1786 and was informed that:

Though I am not at this moment able to state to You the Place to which any Number of the convicts will be sent, I am able to assure you that Measures are taken for procurring the Quantity of Shipping necessary for conveying above a thousand of them [i.e. convicts]....(A)ll the Steps necessary for the removal of at least that number may be completed in about a month.[18]

In fact it took far longer; in August 1786 Lord Sydney, the Home and Colonial Secretary, revealed the plan to the Lords Commissioners of the Treasury:

The several gaols and places for the confinement of felons in this kingdom being in so crowded a state that the greatest danger is to be apprehended, not only from their escape, but from infectious distempers, which may hourly be expected to break out amongst them, his Majesty....has been pleased to signify to me his royal commands that measures should immediately be pursued for sending out of this kingdom such of the convicts as are under sentence or order of transportation.
...his Majesty has thought it advisable to fix upon Botany

35

Landing at Botany Bay, *lithograph, 1786; the satire is directed at English public figures for the Government's decision to found a penal colony at Botany Bay; the figure up to his knees in water and having his pocket picked is King George III.*

Bay... which, according to the accounts given by the late Captain Cook, as well as the representatives of persons who accompanied him during his last voyage.... is looked upon as a place likely to answer the above purposes.[19]

For many years Australian historians assumed that this expedient solution to the prison problem was the sole reason behind the foundation of their new colony; more recently (since the 1950s) a growing argument has developed suggesting a greater political and economic motive. France and Holland were close allies, with powerful trading links with the East; it appeared, to Pitt and Lord Sydney, that the British were in danger of being squeezed out. England badly needed a new strategic sea base and refitting port to strengthen her commercial empire in the East, to protect shipping routes, particularly the China tea trade, and to support, should it be necessary, the empire in India. Flax, for sails, and tall straight pines, for masts, were required to refurbish the fleet – there was no suitable timber in India – and Cook had noted both in abundance on Norfolk Island, 1,000 miles east of Botany Bay.[20]

To head their convict colony the Government selected a semi-retired naval captain, Arthur Phillip, who at the time was farming at Lyndhurst, in the New Forest – a modern tabloid would have had a field-day with headlines – 'King' Arthur and his Convicts. His commission, dated 26 October 1786, was addressed to 'our trusty and well-beloved Captain Arthur Phillip, greeting....'.[21] It appointed him as Governor of the territory called New South Wales, extending from the northern cape (Cape York) at latitude 10° 37' south to the southern extremity or South Cape at 43° 39' south and all of the country inland to the west as far as the 135th degree of longitude; an area considerably larger than that of the whole of Western Europe.

3 FIRST FLEET

In many ways Arthur Phillip was an odd choice to be the Commander-in-Chief of the First Fleet, to become the founder of the colony and New South Wales' first Governor. He was not young, nor well, nor strong, nor commanding in appearance; he was a quiet, unobtrusive sort of man but with hidden qualities which became apparent as he faced first the grinding bureaucracy of the Admiralty and Treasury prior to his departure, and then the gruelling task of total responsibility for the colony of detritus he was instructed to govern.

Arthur Phillip was born in London in 1738; his father, a German immigrant, had taken up the teaching of languages and married a widow – her previous husband, a relation of Lord Pembroke of the British Navy, had died in the war between Spain and Britain. This earlier marriage secured Phillip a place at a school in Greenwich for the sons of naval men killed or drowned in service at sea. As intended he joined the Navy and gained experience in the Merchant Service in the North Atlantic; during the Seven Years' War he served in the Mediterranean and in 1763, as a 25 year old lieutenant, he was placed on the Reserve List of the Navy on half pay – leaving him to be recalled at any moment to take up duty again.

His marriage to Margaret, widow of John Denison, a prosperous London merchant, was a disaster, but through it he took on the management of the family's estates at Vernals Farm and Glasshayes in the New Forest. In 1774, when war broke out between Spain and Portugal, Phillip requested permission from the Admiralty to join Britain's ally, Portugal, and serve in the Portuguese Navy; permission granted, by strange coincidence one of his tasks was to ferry 400 criminals from Portugal to Brazil. The Marquis da Lavradio, Phillip's Commanding Officer in the Portugese Navy, described him as

Captain Arthur Phillip (1738-1814); appointed by the Government to lead the First Fleet to Botany Bay and to become the first Governor of New South Wales. (By courtesy of the National Maritime Museum)

an active and intelligent officer. His health is very delicate but he never complains excepting when he has nothing to do for the Royal Service....He is somewhat self-distrustful, but being an officer of education and principle, he gives way to reason and does not, before doing so, fall into those exaggerated excesses of temper.[1]

Following his recall to service – there is no record of any hesitation on his part before accepting – for the unique task of leading the first convict settlement in New South Wales, Phillip's immediate preoccupation was to badger the Admiralty into providing sufficient equipment and supplies to give his embryonic colony at least a chance of success. Eleven ships were to sail in the First Fleet: two naval ships, HMS *Sirius*, the flagship, and HMS *Supply*, six transports for carrying convicts, *Alexander*, *Scarborough*, *Friendship*, *Prince of Wales*, *Charlotte* and *Lady Penrhyn* and three store ships for carrying supplies, *Fishburn*, *Golden Grove* and *Borrowdale*.[2] Phillip realised that it would take getting on for 18 months for him to obtain anything that was forgotten – by the time he had got a request back to England, and another vessel had returned to Australia – so it was essential to obtain everything that might be needed and to be sure that all was carefully stowed on board.

The first proposed departure date for the fleet was 19 August 1786; the convicts were selected from prisons and hulks all over the country and assembled in the transport vessels at Deptford on the Thames. Phillip clearly took a close interest in the activity and was appalled by the state of many of the convicts; despite his rational argument for men and women skilled in agriculture or construction crafts like carpentry and brickmaking, many were 'ideots and lunaticks', others racked by venereal disease, and pitifully few of them had any useful skills or experience. On 18 March 1787, after a miserable delay through the winter with the convicts holed up and chained beneath the decks, Phillip wrote to Sir Evan Nepean, Under-Secretary of the Home Office:

> The situation in which the magistrates sent the women on board the *Lady Penrhyn* stamps them with infamy – tho' almost naked and so very filthy that nothing but clothing them could have prevented them from perishing.[3]

16 of the prisoners died over that winter and many caught diseases unnecessarily, the transports morosely moored in the grey sludge.

Philip Gidley King (1758-1808); Second Lieutenant on HMS Sirius *in the First Fleet. (By courtesy of the National Maritime Museum)*

Phillip maintained a battery of complaints, not only about the prisoners, for whom he had remarkable sympathy, but also at the poor quality of the tools and equipment being supplied. He found himself busily employed checking and rechecking the stores and ensuring that everything was in good order.

Conditions on board the transports were unbelievably crowded, the *Alexander,* for example, a barque-built ship of 452 tons, 114 feet long and 31 feet wide, carried 195 male convicts; four convicts had to live and sleep in a space 7 feet by 6 feet. On the *Scarborough,* carrying 208 convicts, headroom between decks, where the prisoners were confined for 23 hours out of 24, was 4 feet 5 inches.[4] Tight security added to the claustrophobia; Philip Gidley King, the Second Lieutenant of the

41

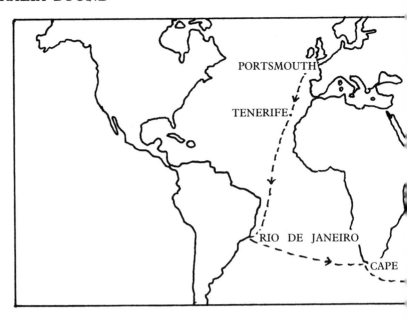

Sirius, born at Launceston, Cornwall, in 1758, of a long established local family, described:

> ..very strong and thick bulkheads, filled with nails and run across from side to side 'tween decks abaft to the mainmast, with loopholes to fire between decks in case of irregularities. The hatches are well secured down by cross-bars, bolts and locks, and are likewise rail'd round from deck to deck with oak stanchions. There is also a barricade of planks about three feet high, armed with pointed prongs of iron....Centinels are placed at the different hatchways, and a guard always under arms on the quarterdeck of each transport in order to prevent any improper behaviour of the convicts'.[5]

On a modern liner approximately 250 tons of ship are allowed per person embarked – in the First Fleet less than three tons of ship were provided.

In March 1887 the Fleet began to reassemble in Portsmouth and to continue loading supplies and convicts; West Country convicts were well represented, the *Charlotte* and *Friendship* had been sent down to Plymouth to collect their charges and to relieve the local hulks and prisons. Amongst those on board were:[6]

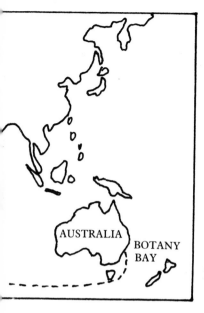

The route of the First Fleet from England to Port Jackson.

Charlotte:

John Arscott, a carpenter from Truro, sentenced on 18 August 1783, to seven years. He later married Catherine Prior (See below).

Mary Bryant/Brand/Broad, from Fowey (Cornwall), convicted at Exeter.

Richard Widdicombe, from Devon – possibly South Brent (See below). He was convicted at Exeter.

John Clarke, a sheep stealer from Exeter – he died of dropsy at Tenerife on the voyage out.

Catherine Prior/Fryer, convicted with Mary Bryant at Exeter.

Margaret Stewart, six bills of indictment were found against her for thefts from several shops in Exeter.

William Bryant, a fisherman from Cornwall.

John Mortimer and his brother **Noah,** from Chagford (Devon); seven years for stealing one wether sheep, value 12s. from John Rowe, and 40lbs of mutton, value 10s., the property of persons unknown.

Edward Westlake, a Devon farmer.

John Small, tried at the Devon Lent Assizes, held at Exeter Castle on Monday 14 March, 1785, for assaulting James Burt in the King's Highway, and violently taking from him against his will one metal watch and Tortoiseshell case value 30s., one pruning knife value 6d., and five shillings; he was sentenced to seven years transportation.

James Underwood, sentenced at New Sarum (Salisbury, Wiltshire) for stealing a ewe.

Alexander:

Joseph Longstreet, sentenced to seven years for stealing a quantity of wool from Benjamin Webb of Melksham (Wiltshire).

Richard Morgan, from the city gaol at Bristol, seven years transportation for stealing a watch and threatening John Trevillian in an attempt to extract a promissory note for £500.

William Okey, a labourer from Painswick (Gloucestershire),

The interior of a convict transport vessel; conditions were very crowded and during stormy weather when the hatches would be battened down for days on end, the atmosphere grew fetid.

death sentence reprieved for burglary from the house of Richard Harwood – he stole three flitches of bacon, six chines of bacon and one bacon spare rib, four loaves of bread, some pigmeal and some hempen cloth.

Edward Risby, a labourer from the Parish of Uley (Gloucestershire), seven years for stealing three yards of broad cloth and two other pieces of cloth.

Richard Smart, seven years for stealing about 30lbs of Hereford wool from the yard next to William Capel's mill in Stroud (Gloucestershire). He died on the voyage.

Scarborough:

John Seymour, committed on 20 March 1786 by Sir William Oglander, being charged with feloniously cutting, lopping and topping a Maiden Ash tree at Beaminster (Dorset). He was ordered to be discharged, but then indicted for felony, found guilty and sentenced to seven years transportation.

James Ruse, a husbandman, from Launceston, Cornwall. (See below)

The Alexander *Transport ship, 1783; the master was Thomas Hart. (By courtesy of the National Maritime Museum).*

In total 736 convicts sailed in the First Fleet; 431 of them had been sentenced for minor thefts, 93 for breaking and entering to steal, 71 for highway robbery and 44 for stealing cattle or sheep. 90 per cent of them were under 35 years old and a half under 25.

While the convicts languished in their cramped quarters, the marines and crews paced the decks preparing for departure after fond farewells ashore. One young officer on HMS *Sirius* wrote home to his father, John Fowell, at Black Hall, near South Brent (Devon):[7]

> Hon'd Father
> I have been in expectation of a Letter from you these several Days and as I am now out of Patience write you a second not that I have any Particular News but that I know it is your desire....We do not expect to sail this Month and I hear in London it is Reported we are not going at all....Nothing at Present makes me the least uneasy except that of Capt. Philip's (sic) not coming down to go to sea as I wish to go as soon as possible as I am all Ready and Clothes weare out laying at the Mother Bank as well as at sea. I should be much obliged to you if you could send me a Pot of Cloted Cream if you could make it convenient. I should think it the best present of the sort you could send me......I have been enquiring about the convicts and have found out Widdicombe he is on board the Charlotte and the Capt. of her has told me if I could Mention any thing he could do for him he wd. do it with pleasure. I told him the man [was of] a good Character...
> Your dutiful son
> Newton Fowell 17 April 1787

At last, on 7 May, Phillip arrived in Portsmouth, still pressing the Admiralty to provide additional necessities – legal papers documenting the crimes of the convicts, clothing for the women he had requested long ago, medical supplies, extra ammunition for the marines, various fresh foods and, most controversial of all, more liquor for the marines.

The crews and marines, bored to death waiting for orders, had become increasingly difficult to control; they slaked their sexual thirsts with the convict women, despite severe lashings if caught, and drew up an ultimatum saying that they felt 'sorely agrieved by finding the intentions of Government to make no allowance of spiritous liquor or wine after our arrival at the intended colony'.

Many of these issues remained unresolved when Phillip, on *Sirius*, gave the order for the Fleet to set off at 4am on Sunday 13 May. His last despatch reflects his relief at finally getting under way – 'All our difficulties are ended'.[8]

Not all officers were happy at the thought of three years away from home; Ralph Clark, a Second Lieutenant on *Friendship*, begged in his diary:[9]

> O gracious god Send that we may put into Plymouth or Torbay in our way down Channell that I may see my dear and fond affectioned Alicia and our Sweet Son before I leave them for this long absents.

That was not to be, the wind was favourable and hurried the vessels on; after 20 days sailing they put in to Tenerife to take on water and fresh vegetables. Marines and convicts alike enjoyed fresh beef (1lb and ½lb per day respectively) and soft bread, a welcome relief from the usual fare of salt pork and hard musty bread; Phillip reported proudly to the Home Office that 'the convicts are not so sickly as when we sailed' and that only eight had died on route.[10]

Newton Fowell took the opportunity of bringing his father up to date with another letter home:[11]

> Hon'd Father,
> We arrived at Santa Cruz last night after a very good passage of only three weeks which we think very tolerable as the *Charlotte* one of the Transports sail very bad indeed and she is a very great hinderence to us...
> On May 20 two Convicts were brought on board us to be punished for Mutiny they had their plan fixed very well but were informed of/ they were to take the Ship in the Night as there was at that time a fair Wind for france most likely they would have landed if possible there – We shall stay here only a few days and then sail for Rio Jenairo on the Coast of Brazils....
> I like Capt Philip (sic) vastly he is very good humoured fine and Chearful, he sent for me today and told me as the first Leiutt. Mr Bradley is to be day Officer I was to take his Watch and do Duty as Acting Lieutt. – tell my Mother in Case of Writing to me not to make a Mistake and Direct Lt. as most likely it is only for a week so you see I am just like a Sheet Anchor used only Particular Cases....
> Santa Cruz, 4 June 1787.

Next stop was Rio de Janeiro. After a voyage of 56 days with stormy seas and deteriorating behaviour on board, they woke up to 'a remarkable fine morning' in Rio on 6 August, and the landscape 'beautiful in the extreme'.[12] While the ships were replenished once again, and exotic delicacies like 'yams, bananas, Guavas, Limes, Lettices, Barangoles and oranges' bought in the local markets, Phillip payed his respects to the Governor, Don Luis de Varconcellos. They stayed nearly seven weeks, with the convicts allowed up on deck to exercise and the officers exploring the city and countryside; Ralph Clark collected butterflies and George Worgan, surgeon on *Sirius*, entertained on his piano. Others eyed the female talent ashore, but were put off by their appalling body odour – 'the use of the cold bath, we found, was wholly unknown to the inhabitants'.[13]

The day before they left, Clark 'brought on board Several Young orange Trees, coffy and Bananas to carry to Botany Bay and sixteen cabbages for the mess'.[14] On 4 September, with clear weather and the wind in the north, the little fleet headed out to sea, cheered by a 21 gun salute from Fort Santa Cruz. Unfortunately the weather broke, and in mid-ocean they were battered and tossed by lashing rain and stormy seas; the heavily laden ships rolled and lurched – in the cabins furniture and utensils were thrown wildly from side to side and with the sea breaking over the ships, the hatches over the convict wards were battened down. On *Friendship* Clark says 'it blowd very hard all night and the ship rould her Gunwale under Several times and a great dele of water went between decks and washt the marines out of ther beds and the Convict Women'.[15] Amidst the confusion, one of the convict women's children, Thomas Mason, died; prayers were read over the child by Henry Lovall, another convict, before the body was 'committed to the deep'.

Their final port of call was at Cape Town; they all arrived safely on 13 October but their welcome was far less cordial than in Rio. The Dutch Governor claimed that he did not have enough food for his own settlement, let alone for supplying this expedition; the bread they bought made them ill and worst of all the port offered little shelter from the violence of the winds. Eventually the Dutch colonial bureaucracy gave way and Phillip was able to obtain supplies; he wrote: 'In the course of a month, the livestock and other provisions were procured; and the ships, having on board not less than 500 animals of different kinds, but chiefly poultry, put on an appearance which naturally enough excited

At Cape Town, the First Fleet took on board a collection of animals to stock the new colony's farms; sheep, cattle and horses were stowed wherever space could be found. Illustrated London News, *6 July 1850.*

the idea of Noah's ark'.[16] The convicts' cells were rearranged to make way for cattle stalls; horses for Phillip were loaded on *Lady Penrhyn*, and 30 sheep were put on board *Friendship*.

All were eager for news from home, but there were few letters waiting for their arrival, so when an English sail was sighted, the *Ranger* out of Falmouth, there was great excitement; she was saluted with 'huzzas' as she passed the *Sirius*, but as she brought scarcely a fist-full of letters, many had to give up hope of hearing from their loved ones for a year or more, until a second fleet should be sent, if ever – such was their imminent isolation.

The last and longest leg of the journey was to prove by far the worst; the voyage took considerably longer than expected because the Fleet met easterlies rather than westerlies for the first week out of Cape Town, and for the last week northerlies prevented them from approaching Botany Bay. Phillip planned to split the Fleet at this point so that he could go ahead and make preparations by setting up a base camp – he tranferred to the swift-sailing *Supply*. Ironically the high seas prevented her from pushing ahead, and even the most sluggish transports kept apace. The storms were terrible; great seas crashed onto the decks and soaked the convicts battened down in their cells; with the hatches closed for long periods of time, the stench below was revolting and there was little chance of the convicts drying off, taking exercise or keeping warm. On *Charlotte*, on 14 November, Catherine Prior, one of the convicts, gave birth to a boy.[17] – she was to marry later, John Arscott, another convict on board.

By Christmas Day, the greatest problem was with the livestock; many hens and sheep had died, so many that it was suspected that they had been poisoned in some way by the Dutch; and supplies of hay, purchased at exorbitant cost in Cape Town, were running out – it was even suggested that the fleet should put in to Van Dieman's Land to cut grass.

The *Supply* managed to push ahead a little in the run up the east coast

The First Fleet in Botany Bay; incredibly after a voyage of over 15,000 miles the eleven ships of the Fleet arrived safely within 48 hours of each other. (By courtesy of the National Maritime Museum).

towards Botany Bay but was frustrated from putting in by the northerly winds and strong currents; on 18 January the wind turned and at last they were able to edge in towards the shore – 'The hills are cloathed with a verdant Wood with many beautiful slopes'.[18] Several natives were seen running about brandishing spears, but by 3pm the *Supply* was safely at anchor and Phillip, together with a party of officers, landed on the north side of the bay. Confronted by a group of natives, Phillip, alone and unarmed, walked towards them, his arms outstretched in friendship, to offer beads – they responded by putting down their spears.

Incredibly, within 48 hours of the *Supply's* arrival the rest of the fleet was safely at anchor in Botany Bay – a great tribute to the captains and crews. The voyage of over 15,000 miles from England had taken eight months and one week – 252 days; only 48 people had died, a remarkably good record compared with that of later convict transports.

Unfortunately, on shore things were not going so well – Phillip found that the supply of fresh water was inadequate, much of the land boggy, there was little useful timber and there were large numbers of natives; pessimistically Clark wrote: 'If we are obliged to settle here, there will not be a soul alive in the course of a year'.[19] But Phillip had already decided to explore elsewhere and with a small party of officers in three boats he headed north following in the wake of Captain Cook.

They eagerly surveyed the shore, hoping to chance upon that ideal spot each had imagined on the journey out – now it had to manifest itself in reality. The first opening they encountered proved to be Port Jackson, noted but unexplored by Cook; as their tiny vessels passed between the headlands Phillip thankfully recorded:[20]

> we...had the satisfaction of finding the finest harbour in the world, in which a thousand sail of the line may ride in the most perfect security...
> The different coves were examined with all possible expedition. I fixed on the one that had the best springs of water, and in which the ships can anchor so close to the shore that at a very small expence quays may be made at which the largest ships may unload.
> This cove which I honoured with the name of Sydney, is about a quarter of a mile across at the entrance, and half a mile in length.

Phillip quickly returned to Botany Bay to instruct the Fleet to follow him back to Port Jackson. On 26 January, the day now observed as

Anniversary Day, 'the English colours were displayed and possession was taken for His Majesty, whose health, with the Queen's, Prince of Wales' and Success to the Colony was drank, a *feu de joie* was fired by the party of Marines and the whole gave 3 Cheers'.[21] Lieutenant Clark was thrilled by the first sight of his new home; he wrote: 'I cannot compair any think to come nearer to it than about 3 miles above Saltash to the Wair – here we make the Ships fast to the Trees on Shore both sides of Governours Cove'.[22]

If ever, the enormity of his task must have hit Phillip at this time, surveying the rocky shore, with no knowledge of what lay beyond; more than a thousand people were to be dependant on his decisions, their life and death lay in his hands. Phillip was a sensitive, compassionate man,

The founding of Australia at Sydney Cove, from the painting by Algernon Talmage, 1937. After landing from the brig Supply *on 26 January 1788, Captain Arthur Phillip (centre) is shown about to propose the health of His Majesty King George III. (By courtesy of John Vivian).*

but he could see that the criminals in his charge would almost certainly put him in a position of having to inflict hard sentences and even execution in order to maintain any semblance of discipline.

Work began immediately; the prisoners disembarked – some of them stepping on dry land for the first time in 12 months, the stores were unloaded, tents pitched, trees cut down. Although no diaries were written by convicts on the First Fleet, some managed to write letters at the end of the voyage which were smuggled back to England by sailors on the returning transports. One extract gives some insight into their feelings:[23]

> I take the first opportunity that has been given us to acquaint you with our disconsolate situation in this solitary waste of the creation. Our passage, you may have heard by the first ships, was tolerably favourable; but the inconveniences since suffered for want of shelter, bedding etc., are not to be imagined by any stranger. However, we now have two streets, if four rows of the most miserable huts you can possibly conceive of deserve that name. Windows they have none, as from the Governor's house etc., now nearly finished, no glass could be spared; so that lattices of twigs are made by our people to complete their places.....As for the distresses of the women, they are past description, as they are deprived of tea and other things they were indulged in on the voyage by the seamen, and as they are all totally unprovided with clothes, those who have young children are quite wretched.

On 6 February, as the last of the women convicts were landed, the blackening skies opened to release a terrible tropical storm. The male convicts, unleashing months of frustration built up throughout their confinement below decks, broke loose from the temporary gaol-yards and into the women's camp. The grog supplies were ransacked and a night of debauchery ensued.

In the morning, Phillip ordered the convicts back to the camp and announced that formal government was established – from henceforth anyone breaking the rules would be punished. With the whole colony present, the Judge-Advocate, David Collins, read His Majesty's Commission and the Act of Parliament for establishing courts in the colony, making it absolutely clear to everyone that Phillip was in charge. Phillip's first speech displayed both his power and his humanity – he would not shirk from imposing the harshest penalties, but he asked the convicts to recognise the new opportunity they all now faced, he appealed to the goodness in each one of them to make the best of the situation and to work for the good of the colony. He encouraged marriage – to bring some sort of stability to the chaotic situation – and offered rewards to those who bent to their tasks with a will.

The convicts responded with alacrity to Phillip's encouragement to marry; in the first week 14 marriages were celebrated and during the second a further ten. John Small, the convict from Devon who had come out on the *Charlotte,* married Mary Parker, a convict on the *Lady Penrhyn,* sentenced to seven years transportation for 'privately stealing' from her employer (she was in service in London), on Sunday 12 October, 1788 – the service was taken by the Rev. Richard Johnson, the chaplain, with Samuel Barnes and Thomas Akers as witnesses. Their first child, Rebekah, was born on 22 September 1789.[24]

The First Fleet arrived with supplies of food to keep the settlement going for two years, but it was intended from the start that every effort should be made for the colony to become self-supporting; land was cleared, gardens dug and the surviving livestock cared for. Captain Cook had noted in his report of 1769 the apparent fertility of Norfolk Island (1,000 miles north-east of Sydney) where pines and wild flax grew in abundance, and Phillip, who had been instructed to form a settlement there 'to prevent its being occupied by any other European power' decided to establish a satellite colony in the hope that its rich soil would provide food for the settlement at Sydney Cove. Lieutenant Philip Gidley King was put in charge, and set off in the *Supply* with six months rations and 24 people, including his mistress, Ann Inett (a convict from Worcestershire), Richard Widdicombe, the Devon convict recommended by Newton Fowell, Edward Westlake, and Noah and John Mortimer, also from Devon and, more particularly, experienced at farm work.

The Norfolk Island settlement was not a great success; the wind and salt-laden air battered the crops and the island was infested with rats which ate the vegetables. The pine trees proved to be useless for masts, and there was no one who knew how to dress flax. King and his cronies were saved by the mutton-bird which was pathetically easy to catch for food, the birds nested on Mount Pitt, the island's highest hill. However the Devon contingent fared well: Widdicombe became Lieut. King's right-hand-man, and helped to quell an insurrection amongst the other convicts; Edward Westlake later received a land grant of 24 acres, and was joined by his wife and children; Noah Mortimer received ten acres and applied for his wife Anne, and children, Thomas (aged six) and Robert (aged four), to be sent out – although there is no record of their arrival; and John Mortimer received 16 acres.[25]

Back at Sydney Cove the work of clearing and building continued. The soil around the Cove was found to be far from satisfactory and Phillip set about exploring inland in the hope of finding an area more suitable for cultivation. The first season's crops were a depressing failure, and stocks of seed were low. Together with the Surveyor-General, Augustus Alt, Phillip chose to establish a second settlement about 16 miles west of Sydney Cove at a place he christened Rose Hill – after Sir George Rose, Secretary to the Treasury (later the name reverted to the aboriginal name Parramatta). Convicts were sent out and the ground cleared for the first shelters. In 1789 a new government farm was commenced here under the superintendence of Edward Dodd, Phillip's private servant, and in November of that year, James Ruse, a convict from Cornwall, was allowed to occupy a farm of his own as an experiment in self-sufficiency.

Ruse's 30 acre property, on the south side of the Barrack Ponds at Parramatta, was known as Experiment Farm; he received the title to the land in April 1791 – the first official land grant to be made. Late in 1790 Ruse told Watkin Tench, a Captain in the Marines, who recorded his account of the First Fleet:[26]

> I was bred a husbandman, near Launceston in Cornwall. I cleared my land as well as I could, with the help afforded me. The exact limit of what ground I am to have, I do not yet know; but a certain direction has been pointed out to me, in which I may proceed as fast as I can cultivate. I have now an acre and a half in bearded wheat, half an acre in maize, and a small kitchen garden. On my wheat land I sowed three bushels of seed, the produce of this country, broad cast. I expect to reap about 12 or 13 bushels. I know nothing of the cultivation of maize, and cannot therefore guess so well at what I am likely to gather. I sowed part of my wheat in May, and part in June. That sown in May has thriven best. My maize I planted in the latter end of August, and the beginning of September. My land I prepared thus: having burnt the fallen timber off the ground, I dug in the ashes, and then hoed it up, never doing more than eight or perhaps nine, rods in a day, by which means, it was not like the government farm, just

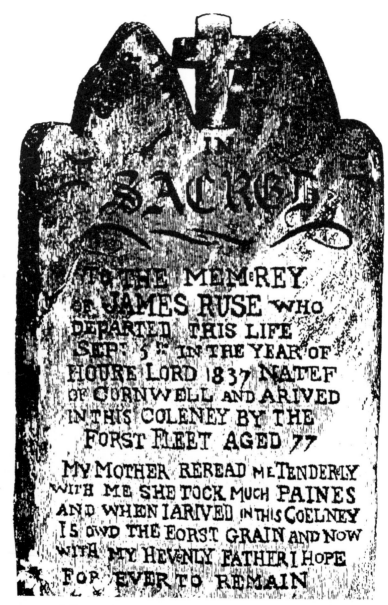

Gravestone of James Ruse from Launceston (Cornwall); a convict in the First Fleet. He was given land at Rose Hill, near Sydney, as an experiment in self-sufficiency and proved so painstaking in his work that Phillip gave him the first official land grant.

scratched over, but properly done; then I clod-moulded it, and dug in the grass and weeds: – this I think almost equal to ploughing. I then let it lie as long as I could, exposed to air and sun; and just before I sowed my seed, turned it all up afresh. When I shall have reaped my crop, I purpose to hoe it again, and harrow it fine, and then sow it with turnip-seed, which will mellow and prepare it for next year. My straw, I mean to bury in pits, and throw in with it every thing which I think will rot and turn to manure. I have no person to help me, at present, but my wife, whom I married in this country: she is industrious. The governor, for some time, gave me the help of a convict man, but he is taken away. Both my wife and myself receive our provisions regularly at the store, like all other people. My opinion of the soil of my farm, is, that it is middling, neither good or bad. I will be bound to make it do with the aid of manure, but without cattle it will fail. The greatest check upon me is the dishonesty of the convicts, who, in spite of all my vigilance, rob me almost every night.

Around Sydney Cove the settlement expanded; Phillip began to plan a city from scratch. He wrote to Lord Sydney:[27]

I have endeavoured to place all public buildings in situations that will be eligible hereafter, and to give a sufficient share of ground for the stores, hospitals etc to be enlarged, as may become necessary in the future. The principal streets are placed so as to admit a free circulation of air, and are two hundred feet wide.

His hopes and imagination fired on the one hand, on the other was the daily drudge of coping with the convicts and their problems. Everyone was entitled to a weekly ration of provisions from the Government Store:

4lbs beef
2lbs pork
2pts dried peas
3pts oatmeal
7lbs hardtack
12oz cheese
6oz butter
¼pt vinegar

for sailors, marines and officers; one third less for male convicts, and two thirds of the male ration for the female convicts. There were of course a number of convicts who had no idea how to make their rations spin out over the week. One man made a load of cakes which he ate immediately – and died the next day; another, in an effort to get money for his return passage to England, sold his rations and died of starvation. Thefts of food were severely punished – by public floggings in the first instance, and death for a second offence.

Understandably, there were few attempts to escape; the odd convict ran off into the bush and usually disappeared amid rumours of cannibalism or murder; some returned to the settlement crazed by starvation and thankful to be back in spite of the punishment they faced. William Bryant and Mary Broad, Cornish convicts on the *Charlotte*, carried out one of the most daring escape bids in 1790 – when together with their two children and seven other convicts they fled in a small boat; they successfully sailed the 3,000 miles or more to the island of Timor. Eventually they were arrested and sent back to Britain; William and the children died during the long voyage. Mary made it and was imprisoned in Newgate, but was freed in 1793 and returned to Cornwall.[28]

Phillip quickly tried to demonstrate his system of morality and justice to the aboriginals, who, needless to say, were fascinated and awed by all the goings on; convicts and marines alike were punished, where possible in front of the natives, for provoking them. In December 1788, on Phillip's instructions, a native was captured in Manly Cove and brought back to Sydney Cove. His name turned out to be Arabanoo and he settled down, apparently quite happily, to live with the white men. Unfortunately he died of smallpox after only a few months and was buried in the Governor's garden; the disease then ravaged the other aborigines in the neighbourhood:

> Soon after (Arabanoo) was taken the Small Pox raged among them with great Fury and carried off great Numbers of them/ every boat that went down the Harbour found them laying Dead on the Beaches and in the caverns of rocks forsaken by the rest as soon as the disease is discovered on them/ They were generally found with the remains of a small Fire on each Side of them and some Water left within their Reach....[29]

Phillip was still keen to establish a language relationship with the natives, so two more natives were 'collected' – Bennelong and Colbee. It was soon discovered that they had enormous appetites, which caused considerable problems when supplies of food for the colony were so miserably low. Colbee escaped shortly after being brought in, but Bennelong lived in the settlement for about six months.[30]

Most of the ships of the First Fleet were despatched, loaded with letters and specimens of flora and fauna, leaving only the *Sirius* and *Supply* to serve the colony; in his reports Phillip stressed their desperate need of supplies of food, seeds, clothes and tools. On 6 March 1790, Phillip sent another batch of people in *Sirius* to Norfolk Island to relieve pressure on the stores in Sydney Cove; but disaster struck – the ship was wrecked on the coast of the Island, and although convicts and sailors managed to scramble ashore many of their provisions were lost.

On Norfolk Island there were now 506 people all surviving on half rations; martial law was imposed to maintain order. Back in Sydney Cove, too, rations were lowered to 2¼lbs flour, 2lbs rice and 2lbs meat a week – it was at this time, it is said, that guests invited to dine at Government House (little more than a shack) were expected to bring their own bread – Phillip had handed over for public use all his own stores and had put himself on the same rations as all the others. Many very ordinary things were in short supply – Newton Fowell wrote home ever so hopefully: 'I should likewise be very thankful for a Couple pair of buckets a few pocket Handkerchiefs and some soap....'[31]

Just to add to Phillip's burden, the Second Fleet arrived on 3 June 1790; the *Lady Juliana* brought 222 women convicts, but no extra provisions, and the news that the *Guardian*, a store ship laden with all the items Phillip had ordered, had been wrecked after hitting an iceberg. The rest of this Fleet had embarked with something in the region of 800 convicts; when they arrived it was found that a quarter of them had died on the journey, and more than half of those that survived were helplessly ill.

Phillip himself was suffering from continual pain in his side; he struggled to continue the administration and it is remarkable that despite everything, he managed to achieve so much. Early in 1791 he asked for relief to return to England for medical attention. Meanwhile shiploads of convicts continued to arrive. The turning point in the fortunes of the colony was undoubtedly the long-awaited arrival of the *Gorgon* – on board was Lieutenant King, who had been sent back to England to make a personal report on the colony, with his new wife,

Anna Josepha, née Coombe, fresh from Hatherleigh (Devon).[32]

In November, Phillip made the decision to resign – apart from medical reasons, he felt that the best contribution he could make was to interview the authorities himself and to make the case that the only hope for the colony was that it should be 'farmed by farmers and emigrants who have been used to labour and who reap the fruits of their own industry.'[33]

The labouriously slow transfer of messages confined Phillip to his post for a further year, the colony struggling on under his jurisdiction; the total population topped 4,500 and more than 1,700 acres were under cultivation. On 10 December 1792, he boarded the *Atlantic* after a farewell given with full honours, by the New South Wales Corps. With him he took two time-expired convicts and two aborigines, Bennelong and Yemmerrawannie.[34]

Back in England, after medical treatment, Phillip attempted to argue his case for free settlers and farmers to be encouraged to go to the colony – without much success; only 20 free settlers migrated before 1800. He returned to duty with the British Navy and in 1798 was put in charge of a sort of maritime 'home guard', the *Sea Fencibles*.

He settled in Bath, Avon, initially taking lodgings in South Parade to see what the Bath waters could do for him[35]; after five years of the company of intransigent marines, bolshy crews and foul-mouthed convicts he clearly longed for the gentility and style of a city renowned for its social graces. In 1806, together with his second wife, Isabella, he moved into 19 Bennett Street, an imposing Georgian mid-terrace residence, opposite the Assembly Rooms and a stone's throw from the Circus and Royal Crescent. Sadly, within a year of his retirement he suffered a severe stroke, which paralysed the right side of his body.

On 31 August 1814, three months after receiving his last promotion, to Admiral of the Blue, he died and was buried at a simple ceremony in the nearby village church of St Nicholas, Bathampton.

For many years the annual commemoration of Phillip's birth was held in London, but since 1946 it has taken place in Bath; in 1975 an Australia Chapel was created in St Nicholas Church, by the architect John Vivian, using Australian materials – Wombeyan marble for the floor and Blackbeam timber for all the joinery; the cross and candlesticks were a gift from the High Commission and the two windows bear the arms of all the Australian States in stained glass.[36] In the afternoon of the commemoration day, a ceremony is held in the splendour of Bath

Abbey, where there is another Phillip Memorial[37] and over which the Australian flag flies.[38]

Many First Fleeters prospered beyond their wildest dreams; having served their term, or gained a 'ticket of leave' by good behaviour they were able to capitalise on the opportunities offered within the colony – one such was James Underwood, sentenced for stealing a ewe at New Sarum, and transported on the *Charlotte*. He set up as a shipwright in partnership with another convict, Henry Kable, and within ten years was running a considerable business in Australia's first private shipyard. By 1806 the firm, Kable and Underwood, owned at least five whaling and sealing vessels; their sloops and schooners traded up and down the coast. In 1807 Underwood returned to England where he persuaded his brother, Joseph, to join him in Australia; they took out a mass of stores and became successful merchants, operating from a warehouse in George Street, where they also had an elegant residence. The brothers continued in partnership, even bringing their mother out for a spell to stay. James was the first person in Australia to receive a distilling licence; he craftily managed to squeeze out his partners before the operation had properly begun, and thus became the sole owner of Australia's first distillery. Eventually he retired to England where he died in 1844 at Tulse Hill, Surrey.[39]

4   HIS NATURAL LIFE

Adieu to Old England
or The Transport's Farewell

(Air: *Native lad*)

Come all you wild young native lads
Wherever you may be,
One moment pay attention
And listen unto me.
I am a poor unhappy soul,
Within those walls I lay
My awful sentence is pronounced,
I am bound for Botany Bay.

I was brought up in tenderness,
My parents' sole delight.
They never could be hapy
But when i was in their sight.
They nourished my tender yrs
And Oft to me would say,
Avoid all evil company
Lest they lead you astray.

My parents bound me prentice
All in fair Devonshire
To a linen Draper,
The truth you soon shall hear.
I bore an excellent character,
My master loved me well,
Till in a harlot's company
Unfortunately I fell.

In the gayest of splendour
I maintained this lofty dame,
But when my money was spent
She treated me with disdain.
She said go robe your master,
He has it in great store,
If some money you don't get
You'll see my face no more.

To her bad advice I yielded
And to my Master went;
To plunder him of what i could,
It was my full intent.
Of costly robes and money too
I took as you shall hear
All from the best of masters,
As to me did appear.

The next robbery i committed,
It was on a gentleman,
Of full 500 sovereigns
He placed them in my hand.
Taken i was for this sad crime,
To Exeter sent me;
The Harlot then forsook me quite
In this extremety.

The assizes then drew near,
Before the Judge i stand.
My prosecutor then swore that
I was the very man.
My aged parents dear, they
So bitterly did cry,
Oh must we with a bleeding heart
Bid our fair boy good bye.

My master and friends
As they stood in the hall,
What floods of tears they shed,
And for mercy did call.
The cruel jade no mercy shew'd
But unto me did say,
My lad you're transported -
And to Botany Bay.[1]

Between 1808 and 1822 more than 500 prisoners were transported to Australia from Ilchester Gaol alone; those whose death sentences had been remitted were, without exception, transported for life, lesser offenders were sentenced to seven years.[2] Throughout the country, all manner of people were sentenced to transportation and in total more than 160,000 men and 25,000 women were banished to Australia between 1788 and 1868, when transportation ceased.

There are few memorials to transported criminals; only pardoned heroes like the Tolpuddle Martyrs, perhaps, deserved to be remembered; but many were sentenced, as described in the previous chapter, for crimes which today would be considered trivial; and others, scarcely able to make ends meet by legal means, turned to petty crime and poaching as a way of life entirely necessary for the support of their families. 'Hunger made people reckless'[3] and to steal a sheep must have been such a temptation; no wonder it was such a common crime.

On the edge of Salisbury Plain at Gore Cross, on the east side of the A360 road between West Lavington and Tilshead, and on Chitterne Down, two monolithic stones were erected with plaques describing the salutary tale of what befell four highwaymen:[4]

> At this spot Mr Dean of Imber was attacked and robbed by four highwaymen in the evening of October 21 1839. After a spirited pursuit of three hours one of the felons, Benjamin Colclough, fell dead on Chitterne Down. Thomas Saunders, George Waters and Richard Harris were eventually captured and were convicted at the ensueing Quarter Sessions at Devizes and transported for the term of fifteen years. This monument is erected by public subscription as a warning to those who presumptuously think to escape the punishment God has threatened against thieves and robbers.

The stone on Chitterne Down marks the spot where Colclough died. The stones were erected in August 1840, in the presence of the organising committee and a large number of spectators; and afterwards the company 'retired to Tilshead Lodge where teas and cakes were provided by ladies of the neighbourhood'.[5]

The three surviving highwaymen were as typical as any that were transported to Australia during this period. Richard Harris was 33 years old, a farm labourer from Cornwall, 5ft 5ins tall, fresh complexioned, with a mole on the joint of his left arm. Thomas Saunders was 5ft 6ins tall and had been a shoemaker in Whitechapel, London – he had dark

The Robbers' stone at Gore Cross, between West Lavington and Tilshead (Wiltshire), marking the spot where Mr Dean of Imber was attacked by highwaymen.

brown hair and a large nose. Saunders was clearly a man who could not be mistaken, for on his left arm were tattoed a flower pot, a mermaid, a fisherwoman, an anchor, the initials 'TB' and several other blue marks. George Waters was 25 years old, half an inch under 6ft, and a farm labourer from Bishopstrow (Wiltshire).[6]

All of them had been convicted before but their crimes are not recorded; Saunders and Waters had both spent a year in prison and Harris had already been transported once before to Bermuda for seven years – no mean feat to be transported twice![7]

The family record for transportation must go to the Billett brothers of North Wraxall (Wiltshire): in 1825 John, aged 26, and William, aged 20, were transported for life for horse stealing; at the same time George, 29, was charged on the oaths of Thomas Perren and others with having feloniously stolen one dark grey mare, one bridle and a saddle, his property at Colerne. A short time later he was charged with stealing another mare, belonging to William Hall of Westport; a younger brother, Edward, 17, was committed for counterfeiting a half-crown and the two of them, George and Edward, shared each others company on the convict ship *Sesostris* which arrived in Sydney in March 1826.[8]

John Western, born on Stepcote Hill, in the slums of Regency Exeter, was only 16 years old when he first faced the city's Quarter Sessions in

Notice on the bridge at Wool (Dorset), threatening transportation to anyone convicted of defacing the bridge.

November 1840; he was charged with 'feloniously stealing eight books value 1/6d each the goods of William Spreat'.[9] His sentence of imprisonment for four months, with hard labour, 14 days solitary, and two whippings clearly did not deter him from continuing his criminal career – only three months after his release he was apprehended at the Royal Subscription Rooms in Northernhay Street. He reappeared before the Court and was found guilty of 'feloniously stealing a handkerchief value 1/0d and a snuff box value 1/0d the goods of Samuel Baker'; he was sentenced to transportation for seven years. After the trial he was taken to Exeter prison where he was put in leg-irons for nearly a year, until he was transferred, by sea from Topsham, to a hulk in Plymouth harbour, to await his transport.

The classic epic novel by Marcus Clarke, *His Natural Life*, recounts the tragic story of Rufus Dawes, wrongly convicted of murder and saved from the gibbet to serve a life sentence in Australia;[10] in real life, Edmund Galley was convicted for the murder of Jonathon May, a farmer from Sowton Barton near Dunsford, at Moretonhampstead Fair in 1835; at the time there was sufficient doubt about the case that the Home Secretary commuted the death penalty to transportation for life. In 1877, after more than 40 years in New South Wales, Galley wrote to a solicitor stating that he was now a respectable inhabitant in the district of Binalong and pleaded for his name to be cleared. After continued pressure and a nationwide petition Her Majesty granted Galley a free pardon and a sum of £1,000 was collected and sent to him as compensation.[11]

The removal of prisoners from the courthouse or gaol to their transport ship or hulk was a tricky business; the prisoners, all too aware of their fate, judged – quite correctly – that this was their last chance to make a desperate bid for freedom before being launched into the unknown on the high seas, where their inexperience and uncertainty rendered them almost helpless.

Prisoners sentenced at Dorchester were held in Dorchester Gaol until a convenient number were ready to be moved to Portsmouth for embarkation. They had to walk – in chains – following the route of the present A35 and A31; their first day's march, of about 14 miles, brought them to a point about five miles west of Wimborne Minster; here at the Red Signpost[12] they were turned right down a lane towards Bloxworth. The signpost, it is said, was originally painted red to distinguish it for the guards, most of whom would have been illiterate. The prisoners spent an uncomfortable night in an old brick-built barn, all chained to a central post, which reached to the roof.[13] The barn, built like a prison with narrow slits for windows and heavy studded oak doors, was partly destroyed by a fire in 1935, but the farm retains the name 'Botany Bay Farm' to this day.

From the Somerset County Gaol in Ilchester prisoners sentenced to transportation were delivered to various hulks or transport ships:[14]

Ports	Hulks	Transports
Chatham	Garrymede	
Gosport	York and Laurel	
Portsmouth	York, Laurel, Captivity, Portland	
River Thames	Retribution and Justitian	Minstril
Sheerness	Bellerophon	
Woolwich	Mary Ann	Canada

The Red Signpost on the A31 where convicts, marching to Portsmouth to board a hulk or convict transport, were turned right towards Bloxworth, to spend the night in a barn.

Illustration of the 'van' used to transport prisoners from Wilton Gaol (Taunton) to Portsmouth. (Somerset County Record Office).

The distances being that much greater, they were moved in a specially designed horse-drawn 'van'. The specifications of one such vehicle were drawn up by James Jacobs, a Taunton Coach builder, in 1820, for Wilton Gaol, Taunton.[15] The van, painted Canary yellow, included 'Venitian (sic) blinds in the sides....two pistol cases and seats fix(ed) on the back for the Guards..' and it was to be built for a price of £95.

In spite of the care taken over the construction of these vans and the strict supervision of the 'transports', as the prisoners sentenced to transportation were called, at least one escape plot proved successful, if only for three of the prisoners involved. A week after the incident, on 18 May 1835, the Master of the Ilchester Gaol, William Hardy, gave evidence that:[16]

> 15 prisoners were being conveyed to the hulks at Portsmouth-...that [he] left the jail at five o'clock in the morning with the prisoners in the van...with three guards...before getting up to his usual seat he asked the Turnkey, Richard Pike, if everything was right and on his replying that it was he got up in front of the van...and proceeded on the journey....all went well until they reached Tottern [Totton – on the western outskirts of South-

ampton] where at about one o'clock on a sudden he heard a terrible shouting which he could not understand. He fancied that they had run over some one. Upon looking back he discovered his son and Edward Pike in pursuit of two men, that he called to the post boys who were driving at the rate of about 7¼ miles an hour but before they could pull up they must have proceeded about 50 yards further when....the guard with him got down and on looking under the van discovered a hole in the bottom of the van. [He] then secured the elder Rose [one of the prisoners] who had escaped from the van and put him in the van again, upon turning round he saw Edward Pike coming with Bluford [another prisoner] whom he took from Pike and sent Pike off after the other men who had escaped; he placed Bluford in the van, placing his guard, Mr.Longstaff, in the van also armed with a blunderbuss that shortly after Griffiths another transport was brought back by James Hardy and Edward Pike...

Further investigation of the hole suggested to William Hardy that 'the greater part of what was necessary to enable them to escape was done in the prison'. The other guards were examined and gave sworn statements – one of them was William's son, James, and another, Edward Pike, was the son of the Turnkey.

The documents reveal that James Rose (the son of the 'elder Rose' refered to above) was the ringleader of a gang of 'notorious housebreakers'; he had been sentenced, together with Chas. Lewis and Chas. Lucas who also escaped with him, for robbing Mr Young's pawnbroker's shop in Bath. A few days before the escape Rose's mother had visited the prison and was found to be carrying a box containing 'razors and other instruments' which were taken from her.

Richard Pike swore that he had carefully 'ironed them [the prisoners] in the presence of the jailor rivetting each (basil?) on the leg himself' and in the van, he had 'fastened [a chain] at the head of the van through each man's leg chain...and passed the end of the chain through a hole in the bottom of the van and locked it on to the step'.

Such incidents were rare. Most transports arrived with depressing regularity to be deposited in a hulk or to proceed straightway, if they were so lucky, to their transport ship. Some prisoners spent months, or even years, in the hulks – Edmund Galley, for example, spent two and a half years in the prison hulks at Woolwich, before embarking on a transport ship bound for Sydney in 1839.[17]

Waiting in the transport vessel provided a last chance for messages to be got back to wives and sweethearts; one of the 'Swing' protestors from Wiltshire, Peter Withers, managed to write to his wife, Mary Ann, from the convict ship *Porteus,* moored at Spithead, in April 1831:[18]

My dear wife belive me my hart is almost broken to think I must lave you behind. O my dear what shall I do i am all most destracted at the thoughts of parting from you whom I do love so dear. Believe me My Dear it Cuts me even to the hart and my dear Wife there is a ship Come into Portsmouth harber to take us to New Southweals.....it is about four months sail to that country But we shall stop at several cuntreys before we gets there for fresh water I expects you will eare from me in the course of nine months....you may depend upon My keeping Myself from all other Woman for i shall Never Let No other run into my mind for tis onely you My Dear that can Ease me of my Desire. It is not Laving Auld england that grives me it is laving my dear and loving Wife and Children, May God be Mersyful to me.

We ears we shall get our freedom in that Country, but if I gets my freedom evenso i am shore I shall Never be happy except I can have the Pleshur of ending my days with you and my dear Children, for I dont think a man ever loved a woman so well as I love you.

My Dear I hope you will go to the gentlemen for they to pay your Passage over to me when I send for you. How happy I shall be to eare that you are a-coming after me....Do you think I shall sent for you except i can get a Cumfortable place for you, do you think that I wants to get you into Troble, do you think as I want to punish my dear Children? No my dear if I can get a cumfortable place should you not like to follow your dear Husband who lovs you so dear?

There was no reply from Mary Ann and two years later Withers was writing to his brothers from Van Dieman's Land: 'I have sent two letters to My Wife and Cant get heny Answer from her Wich Causeth me a great deal of unhapyness for i think she have quite forgotten me an i think she is got Marred to some other Man, if she is pray send me word'. But there was still no response, and 11 years were to pass before Mary Ann at last wrote to her husband – in great distress and begging to be reconciled. It was too late, she received the news that Peter had married again to a 'staidy vertus Woman'.[19]

Once the transports were at sea, conditions on board were much like those of the First Fleet; but they could vary dramatically from ship to ship, and from captain to captain, and nothing of course could determine the weather nor the length of the voyage. Between 1795 and 1801 an average of nearly one in ten convicts died on the voyage, but great improvements were made so that between 1801 and 1812 only one in 46 died[20] – every vessel had to carry a surgeon who was charged with ensuring the cleanliness of the ship, treating the sick and visiting all the convicts to check their well-being. He had the power to issue not only medicines, but also extra rations, should any sick person be in want of greater nourishment. The best incentive of all was a gratuity, to the surgeon, of 10s. 6d. for every convict landed safely in New South Wales. Similarly the master received a bonus of £50 for satisfactory conduct.[21]

One group of convicts went so far as to write a letter of thanks to a ship's surgeon, E.F.Bromley, which was produced as evidence to the Select Committee on the State of Gaols in 1819[22] Nevertheless, conditions could never be said to have been luxurious:

> Two rows of sleeping-berths, one above the other, extend on each side of the between-decks of the convict-ship, each berth being six feet square, and calculated to hold four convicts, every one thus possessing eighteen inches space to sleep in, – and ample space too! The hospital is in the fore-part of the ship, with a bulk-head across separating it from the prison, having two doors with locks to keep out intruders; while a separate prison is built for the boys, to cut off all intercourse between them and the men....Scuttle-holes, to open and shut for the admission of air, are cut along the ship's sides; a large stove and funnel placed between-decks for warmth and ventilation; swing stoves and charcoal put on board, to carry into damp corners;......Each is allowed a pair of shoes, three shirts, two pair of trowsers, and other warm clothing on his embarkation, besides a bed, pillow and blanket – while Bibles, Testaments, prayer-books and psalters are distributed among the messes.[23]

Some of the female convicts suffered the most appalling degradations:

> ..the master stript several of them and publickly whipped them; that one young woman, from ill treatment, threw herself into the sea and perished; that the master beat one of the women that lived with me with a rope with his own hands till she was much bruised

72

in her arms, breasts, and other parts of her body.....the youngest and the handsomest of the women were selected from the other convicts and sent on board, by the order of the master, the king's ships.....for the vilest purposes.[24]

On arrival at their destination, the convicts were despatched to work; either they joined a government work gang or they were assigned to work for a particular individual who had satisfied the Governor or a magistrate that they were responsible and (reasonably) honest citizens. Each convict was issued with a coarse woollen jacket, a waistcoat of yellow (hence the nickname 'canaries') or grey cloth, a pair of duck trousers, worsted stockings, a pair of shoes, two cotton or linen shirts, a neck handkerchief and a woollen cap or hat.[25]

Convict labour was imperative to allow the colony to operate and to develop; all clearing and construction work was carried out by convicts – they worked in gangs under an overseer, and with a superintendent in charge of two or three gangs – even the superintendents were convicts, those who had a clean record and showed themselves capable. The gangs worked from six in the morning till three in the afternoon, with 'the remainder of the day allowed to them, to be spent either in amusement

A Chain Gang, from a print in James Backhouse's Narrative of a visit to the Australian Colonies, *London, 1843.*

or profitable labour for themselves'.[26] As time went on, working for the government gangs, particularly on the roads, became a punishment for an offence committed in the colony – then the gang would work in chains, from six until six, with no time for profit or amusement. Convicts with skills were usually retained in the service of the government, mechanics and engineers were in particularly short supply.

In 1803, during the Governorship of Philip Gidley King, Van Dieman's Land was occupied as a secondary convict settlement; in a letter to Eric Nepean (Under Secretary in the Colonial Office) on 9 May 1803, King explained:[27]

> My reasons for making this settlement are: the necessity there appears of preventing the French gaining a footing on the East side of these Islands; To divide the Convicts: To secure another place for procuring timber, with any other natural production that may be discovered and found useful; The advantage that may be expected by raising Grain; and to promote Seal Fishery.

King appointed John Bowen, a naval officer from Ilfracombe, Devon, recently arrived in the colony on the convict transport *Glatton*, to lead the new settlement, promoting him to the rank of Commander. Bowen, just 23 years old, found himself in charge of 21 male and three female convicts, a handful of free settlers and a guard of New South Wales Corps. He sailed up the Derwent estuary and pitched camp, complete with a pair of 12-pounder carronades, at a spot on its eastern shore which he named Risdon.[28] Bowen loved the place and the beautiful scenery of the Derwent estuary which reminded him of a nobleman's park in England rather than an uncultivated wilderness. But just as he was about to sow seed and lay plans for a future town, his peace was interrupted by the arrival of two ships bringing David Collins and his party from Port Phillip.

David Collins, previously Judge Advocate in New South Wales under Governor Phillip, had been sent as Lieutenant-Governor to establish a settlement at Port Phillip Bay (Victoria); dissatisfied with conditions there he decided to make for Sullivan's Cove on the Derwent – the settlement which was later to become Hobart Town – with orders to supersede Bowen. In August 1804 Bowen left, and just six months later he sailed home to England. Early settlers were encouraged to Van Dieman's Land by free grants of land, a minimum of 320 acres and more 'in proportion to their means'. Convicts were needed to build roads, break up the soil and provide the necessary labour to establish a successful colony; initially they were transferred from Norfolk Island, but soon others began to arrive direct from England.

The darker side to life in Van Dieman's Land grew from rumours and stories about the horrific penal camps for 'secondary' offenders – those convicts who committed further crimes either on the voyage out or whilst serving their term in the colony; Macquarie Harbour on the remote west coast, Maria Island on the east coast, and later Port Arthur on the Tasman Peninsula were all such places. There, prisoners were put to incessant back-breaking labour, sometimes shackled by irons; they were brutalised by terrible floggings and saw only one another and their guards. Few accounts have survived of precisely what the conditions really were like, but the reputation of the places was fuelled by descriptions like this from *His Natural Life*:[29]

Three wooden staves, seven feet high, were fastened together in

A convict bound to the 'triangle' receiving his lashes – in this case before being hanged; a magistrate on the right remarks: 'I will give the damned wretch a hundred lashes and send him to be hanged'. The hangman by the gallows replies: 'It's complete butchery but I must do it, I suppose'.

the form of a triangle. The structure looked not unlike that made by gipsies to boil their kettles. To this structure Kirkland was bound. His feet were fastened with thongs to the base of the triangle, his wrists, bound above his head, at the apex. His body was then extended to its fullest extent, and his white back shone in the sunlight. During his tying up he had said nothing – only when Troke roughly pulled off his shirt he shivered.

'Now, prisoner,' said Troke to Dawes, 'do your duty.'.....
Rufus Dawes lifted the cat, swung it round his head, and brought its knotted cords down upon the white back.....'Wonn!' cries Troke.....The white back was instantly striped with six crimson bars.........'Ten!' cried Troke...The lad's back, swollen into a hump, now presented the appearance of a ripe peach which a wilful child has scored with a pin.

One enthusiast for the carefully graded system of punishments and limited rewards was the Lieutenant Governor of Van Dieman's Land from 1824 to 1836, at the height of the oppressive scheme – Colonel George Arthur. He was born at Norley House, Plymouth, in 1784. Before taking up his posting he made sure that he was to have full authority in the sub-colony; he was determined to raise the moral tone of Van Dieman's Land and as a devout evangelical Calvinist he believed that the only means of salvation was through 'Christ crucified and faith in Him'; the heart of every man, he thought, was 'desperately wicked'.[30] 'Convicts', he wrote to the Colonial Office 'should be kept rigidly at the spade and pick-axe and wheel barrow....from morning till night, although the immediate toil.. be the only beneficial result of their labour'.[31] Colonel Arthur, it must be said, promoted separation and solitary confinement rather than flogging; after a few weeks following the 'Silent System' any convicts who persisted in shouting or disturbing the peace in any way were removed to a 'dumb' cell – here an intricate arrangement of doors and total darkness ensured their absolute isolation; ventilation came through a high grating and they were fed on bread and water.[32]

The most shocking tales to come out of Van Dieman's Land, though, are not those of the punishments of convicts, but the appallingly inhuman treatment of the aboriginals. By 1830 a healthy population of some 20,000 natives had been decimated by disease and slaughter to 2,000. As a culmination of atrocities Governor Arthur ordered a line of armed men to drive the survivors into Tasman's Peninsula where they

Colonel George Arthur, Lieutenant Governor of Van Dieman's Land from 1824-36; he was born in 1784 at Norley House, Plymouth (Devon).

could be confined and controlled; but after six weeks they found that their human net contained only an old woman and a sick man. George Augustus Robinson then offered himself for the task of overseeing the remaining natives who could be captured and deposited on Bruni Island (off the south east coast of Van Dieman's Land); this plan proved equally disastrous for the Tasmanians and by the 1860s, the whole race had been obliterated. Robinson later retired to Bath (Avon).[33]

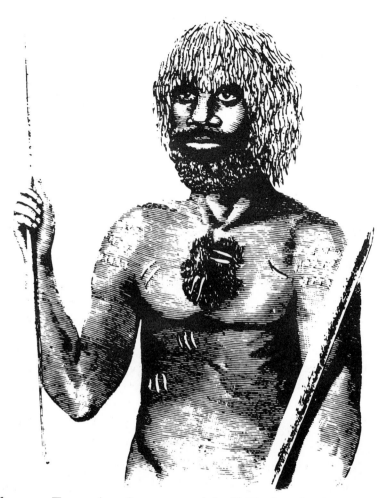

Alphonse, a Tasmanian, from a portrait by T.Napier; the Tasmanian race was wiped out within 70 years of the first permanent European settlement in Van Dieman's Land.

All convicts transported to Van Dieman's Land were not, of course, subjected to secondary punishment. Most were assigned to work on farms, and when assignment was abolished in 1839, a 'probation' system was introduced whereby satisfactory service in a 'probation gang' was rewarded by eligibility to work for wages which were placed to the convict's credit until a ticket-of-leave was finally issued.[34]

Tickets-of-leave could be granted by the governor, and were, more or less, conditional pardons – in 1835, a convict transported for seven years could expect to be released after only four years (only two years for women convicts); one transported for 14 years, after six years (three years for women); and even those with sentences for life would normally be freed at the end of eight years (only four years for women); of course such an indulgence was dependant on good behaviour, and it seemed to provide just the sort of incentive necessary to spur the convicts towards self-improvement. Such apparent leniency towards the female convicts aimed to discourage them from turning, or returning, to prostitution. Ticket-of-leave men found no difficulty in obtaining work at wages far higher than they could ever have expected back home; and with their experience in the colony, they were frequently preferred to lately-arrived emigrants.[35] The better educated were snapped up to become superintendents of estates, clerks to bankers, lawyers and shopkeepers, and tutors in private families.

Ticket-of-leave holders, though, were not entitled to move about freely; they were usually confined to a particular district and they were certainly not free to leave the colony, nor, perish the thought, to return to England.

Back in England various arguments were raging against transportation as a punishment for criminals; despite the very real terror transportation sparked in the minds of the poor – as demonstrated in the lines of the popular song quoted at the start of this chapter – a contrary view was voiced from time to time, as here, by Archbishop Whately in 1833:[36]

To the great bulk of those...who are sentenced to transportation, the *punishment* amounts to this, that they are carried to a country whose climate is delightful, producing in profusion all the necessaries and most of the luxuries of life; – that they have a certainty of maintenance, instead of an uncertainty; are better fed, clothed, and lodged, than (by *honest* means) they ever were before; have an opportunity of regaling themselves at a cheap rate with all the luxuries they are most addicted to; and if their conduct is not intolerably bad, are permitted, even before the expiration of their term, to become settlers on a fertile farm....Whatever other advantages this system may possess, it certainly does not look like a very terrific punishment.

Sir William Molesworth St Aubyn, on the other hand, from Pencarrow

(Cornwall), campaigned for the abolition of transportation for very different reasons; in 1837 he was invited by the Home Secretary, Lord John Russell, to chair the Select Committee on Transportation; in a private letter dated 5 April 1837 Russell wrote:[37]

> My statement with respect to transportation was, I believe, that if allowed to continue to the extent to which in the present system it would in natural course be carried it would create the 'most depraved community that ever existed in the world'.

Sir William was clearly appalled by the gross inhumanity of the punishment and the Committee reported that tickets-of-leave and the assignment of convicts had become matters of favour and therefore open to abuse; 'talented' convicts, whatever their crime, were quickly picked out for skilled work, leaving others, whose crimes may have been far less, to hard labour; the report was critical of Sir George Arthur for advocating the treatment of convicts as 'slaves' and it described the punishments meted out to second offenders as belonging 'to a more barbarous age'. The Select Committee recommended the discontinuance of transportation on the grounds of such abuses and of expense; 'home confinement', it claimed, would cost less, require less guards, be more immediately under the eyes of the Government and public, and would impose a greater impression on other criminals.[38]

Sir William's ideas were too radical for his day, but he continued to make his case and supported the ideas of Edward Gibbon Wakefield for assisted emigration for free settlers funded by the sale of colonial land.[39] Wakefield encouraged him to consider seeking appointment as Governor of New South Wales, but he never took up the suggestion, and later in life, as Secretary of State for the Colonies in 1855, it is likely that his influence would have speeded the end of transportation had not his untimely death prevented it.

Ironically there are stories that support Archbishop Whately's view: the Austin family history, for example, *Convict by Choice* by J.Marjorie Butler[40], recounts the story of two young men from Somerset, who, it appears, elected to be transported as a way of getting a free passage to Australia in the early years. James Austin and John Earle, cousins, from Baltonsborough, were both younger sons of tenant farmers and as such could not expect to be set up with farms of their own in England. In 1802 they were convicted at the Quarter Sessions in Wells for stealing 100 pounds in weight of honey and six straw bee hives from Peter Higgens –

Peter Higgens was James Austin's uncle. Transported to Van Dieman's Land for seven years, James and John ultimately prospered way beyond anything they could possibly have imagined – they co-managed and owned the ferry across the Derwent River, where, on either side they built fine houses and became wealthy merchants and farmers. So successful were they that other members of their families in Somerset, and friends from the district, came out to join them.[41]

The Austins and Earles, though, were exceptions, who through their bravery and determination achieved the goal they desired; for the rest, transportation was effective because it removed the problem just about as far away as was possible and it was certainly a terrible punishment. Whether or not it had any remedial effect on the convicts is difficult to judge – the examples of those who made good are perhaps given disproportionate weight against the mass who continued to live on the fringe of the law.

The British public, always entertained by stories of horror and gore, was, understandably, awed by tales of transportation. Towards the end of the nineteenth century an 'original Australian convict ship' was exhibited at the Barbican, Plymouth; the advertisment claimed '72 original cells intact, wax prisoners within, hundreds of prison punishments and curios'.[42] Visitors flocked to pay the admission price of 6d. for adults and 3d. for children. Earlier, the story of convict piracy on the *Cyprus*, bound for Van Dieman's Land, was dramatised for the London stage.[43] Interestingly the story includes mention of a convict named Popjoy or Popjay who was on the ship when it was taken in Recherche Bay, but refused to take part in the capture. When the convicts eventually made landfall, in China, Popjay did everything he could for the officers, crew and soldiers. Ultimately he received a free pardon for his good conduct and returned to England. A convict by the same name, Popjay (could they be one and the same?), is believed to have returned home to the village of Wylye (Wiltshire); he arrived back, about 1805, in great style and stayed at the Bell Inn, next to the church, travelling in a carriage and giving every appearance of affluence. He discovered that his mother and sister had been buried in paupers' graves, so arranged with the Rector, the Reverend John Dampier, to have their bodies exhumed and reinterred in a magnificent tomb, complete with fine masonry and decorative iron railings. However when the bills began to arrive Popjay had gone. There is a local tradition that the rector subsequently paid the bills and that he himself was buried in the tomb.[44]

The Popjay tomb at Wylye (Wiltshire). (By courtesy of Mrs Morris of Wylye and the Salisbury Journal and Times Series).

5 TRANSPORTATION

In 1828, at the Exeter Assizes, William Stanbury, married with four children, was convicted, with several others, of larceny; he was sentenced to three months hard labour and a whipping.[1] Soon after his release, William was at it again – in the parish of Kingsteignton, near Newton Abbot, Devon, on 16 April in the same year, he stole a cart mare worth £10, knowing it to be the property of William and James Couch of Bellamarsh. He was returned to Exeter Gaol to await his trial.

The Exeter Flying Post reported on Monday 4 August that William Stanbury had been sentenced to death by hanging; his age was given as 24 years, although he was actually 42.[2] Justice Littledale had clearly had a busy day – three other men were given the death sentence: Thomas Haydon, a 19 year old ploughman, for housebreaking and stealing some thread; and the Cording brothers, Thomas (21 years old, also a ploughman) and Samuel (a woolcomber aged 24) – they had broken into a house at Clayhidon (Devon) and stolen 50 yards of printed cotton, ten yards of calico, and ten silk and ten cotton handkerchiefs and other goods. A fourth man, Thomas Sanders, a basket maker, was tried and convicted on the same occasion for petty theft and sentenced directly to 14 years transportation – the others had their death sentences commuted to transportation for life.[3]

All five men were carted off to a prison hulk where they waited ten months – labouring on the wharves. William's prison report stated that his behaviour was 'good'[4]. They left England on the York, on 30 April 1829, bound for Van Dieman's Land. The York, loaded with 192 male convicts, was making her first voyage as a convict ship; the master was John Moncrief and the surgeon-superintendent, responsible for the health and conduct of the prisoners, was Dr Andrew Henderson – himself making his first voyage as surgeon on a convict ship.

Their journey was uneventful until 17 August, just 11 days before Hobart Town was reached, when Andrew Henderson recorded in his journal that William Stanbury 'Complained last night of severe pains in his shoulders, back and legs, says he is subject to Rheumatism in damp weather....This morning complaints much the same....his diet Tea, Sago'.[5] The following day William's pains were very severe 'in every part of his body, especially in the knees and shoulders.... Tongue whitish....Pulse good'. Rice was added to his diet on 20 and 21 August, and his 'pains much relieved, mouth affected by the Calomel (a mercurous chloride purgative)... complaining of nausea'.

By the time the *York* reached Hobart Town William was suffering severely from Rheumatism and dysentery; he was not moved from the ship for three days, whilst his diet was fortified with fresh mutton and broth, and then he was transferred to the Colonial Hospital, at the corner of Liverpool and Argyle Streets. As the convicts were disembarked, full details were taken of their place of birth, family, trade, and criminal record; although William was in hospital, his record was dutifully completed:[6]

Trade:	farm labourer and ploughman
Height:	5' 4½"
Age:	40
Complexion:	dark
Eyebrows:	dark brown
Head:	round
Eyes:	hazel
Hair:	dark brown
Nose:	short
Whiskers:	dark brown
Mouth:	medium width
Visage:	oval
Forehead:	perpendicular, wrinkled
Native place:	Plimpton May (Plympton St Mary), Devonshire

He was allotted the convict number 1022.

Most convicts, at this time, were assigned to work for various officials or settlers, the nature of their work dependant on their record and on previous experience. It is likely that, once he had recovered, William was assigned to a settler in the vicinity of Hobart Town; unlike his compatriots from Devon, William was an exemplary convict – no charges of misbehaviour were laid against him. Thomas Cording, the best behaved of the other four, received 30 lashes for 'Neglect of Duty and insolence'; Thomas Haydon had nine charges laid against him, including 'Insolence and disobedience' and 'Allowing persons to trespass on his Master's premises without leave at 11 o'clock last night and treating them with his Master's provisions' in 1831 – his offences earned him a total of 140 lashes and two months' hard labour in one of the chain gangs. Both Samuel Cording and Thomas Sanders appear to have been regular offenders – Cording was frequently charged with drunkenness and absenting himself from work, and Sanders, too, was convicted on similar charges and was committed, for a period, to the Hobart Penitentiary.[7]

In 1834 William Stanbury was working in the vicinity of Brighton, north of Hobart; in 1837 he was granted a 'ticket-of-leave' – allowing him the right to earn his own living and to choose his own master, wear his own clothes, and to have access to any money he earned. Life-term convicts were usually only awarded a 'ticket' after serving a minimum of eight years of their sentence, with no record of misdemeanors. With a 'ticket', the convict could move about the colony, within certain restrictions, but he could not leave it, and he was still, legally, a convict.

Four years later, William received his conditional pardon (no. 3097), 'conditional' because it guaranteed all privileges except the right to

William Stanbury's convict record from the Archives Office, Tasmania – from Branching Out *by Neil Thomas, 1981.*

return to England; it is interesting to note that the convict Thomas Cording received a similar pardon on the same day. William went to work for George Armytage, a prominent settler who had emigrated from Derbyshire in 1815, employed as an agricultural jack-of-all-trades at a place called Bagdad, north of Brighton.

In 1843 William applied for a further pardon to allow him to return to England, presumably he hoped to be reunited with his family; his name was recommended to the Queen for a Free Pardon in an application dated 17 December 1844 – such documents were always a matter of grace and ratified under the Great Seal. After nearly a year he received notification that his pardon had been granted, but it still did not allow him to return to Europe.[8]

Like many others, William not only longed to return to England, but also to escape the island to which he had been sentenced; unable to go home, he opted for South Australia – a new colony, only recently founded, on lines very different to those of New South Wales and Van Dieman's Land. In South Australia there were no convicts; the land was sold to English landowners and the revenue used to convey labourers and an industrious middle class to the colony. William sailed from Launceston to Port Adelaide on 14 April 1846 in the *Julia*.[9]

William purchased a block of 83 acres, at Berry Hill, on section 6178, in the Hundred of Talmuga, paying just £1 per acre; little is known of his activities, but presumably all went well as he was joined by his daughter, Elizabeth, from England, and her husband, Richard Sandercock in 1853. That same year a stone house was built at Berry Hill, and Richard and Elizabeth rented some of the land off William to start their own farm.

William died at Gumeracha on 4 April 1858 aged about 75, his estate was valued at £300.[10]

John Western's experiences were pretty similar – sentenced to seven years at Exeter, he arrived in Hobart Town on the *Susan* on 24 July 1842. His behaviour as a convict seemed to deteriorate: for the first five months he was described as 'good', by January 1843 'tolerable', and then on 13 January he was found guilty of 'misconduct with three others in violently assaulting a prison officer' and sentenced to 12 months hard labour in chains'.[11] – 'as severe a one [punishment] as could be inflicted on man'.[12] He was sent to Impression Bay and employed on tree clearance and road construction – some of the hardest work. But even there he did not behave himself and within five weeks of his transfer he was ordered an extension of three months for disobedience; 12 weeks later he was given 25 lashes for having three files in his possession.

After further punishments, he was eventually released to be indentured as a servant to Mr J. Aldridge, of Liverpool Street, Hobart Town; in June 1847, with a good report, he achieved his 'ticket-of-leave'.

He met up with Lucy Williamson, the 19 year old daughter of a free settler from Kent, with a good business in Hobart Town; the family, understandably, opposed their friendship and when a baby was produced on 1 December 1850, the couple were forbidden to marry. Once Lucy was 21, the marriage went ahead with a ceremony in St David's Church, Hobart Town; John, unable to write his name, signed the marriage register with a cross; he was described as 'dealer'.[13]

John, Lucy and their daughter, also Lucy, moved to Victoria, lured by the booming trade around the goldfields; they set up a store and prospered. John was able to invest in property in Melbourne and Sydney and in later life became known as 'honest John'[14].

John Western died in Sydney in February 1893, his will provided generously for his grandchildren, and he even remembered his brothers back in Exeter, James and Thomas, and William, who had moved to Liverpool – they were to be given an allowance of 8s. a week. John's tombstone in Gore Hill Cemetery, Sydney, bears the inscription:[15]

We cannot tell who next may fall
Beneath thy chastening rod.
One must be first, but let us all
Prepare to meet our God.

Convict Tales:

Francis Howard Greenway (1777-1837)

There can be few criminals, anytime or anywhere, to be honoured in their penal settlement by having their portrait engraved on the national paper currency, but just so, Australia acknowledges the convict-architect Francis Greenway.

The son of John Greenway and Mary (née Tripp), Francis was christened in Mangotsfield church, on the edge of Bristol, on 20 November 1777; his family were stone masons and he trained as a painter and architect in Bristol and London.[1]

Francis Howard Greenway, the convict-architect from Bristol; the 'Father of Australian architecture'.

In 1805 he joined his two brothers in establishing at Clifton (Bristol) a firm that undertook extensive speculative building from his designs; one of his projects, still standing, was the Clifton Hotel and Assembly Rooms in the Mall – a local newspaper reported:[2]

> The foundations for a new Assembly Room is already begun at the East end of the Mall at Clifton; the design, by Mr Greenway,

The Assembly Rooms in the Mall, Clifton, Bristol. Greenway was working on this building when he was sentenced, for fraud, to be transported.

Architect, of this city does great credit to his abilities, and will be a handsome public building, and will do honour to the liberality and taste of those who have patronised and subscribed to it.

A more recent critic was less impressed:[3]

The frontispiece is a big stone-faced building on the east side in which, in spite of exclusively classical motifs, the desire for variety has certainly defeated the rules of classical composition. In the centre rusticated basement, and then six giant attached Ionic columns and squeezed between two pairs of them two odd oriel windows[4]. Heavy attic storey and pediment on this. Then quieter slightly recessed ranges of four bays (of which two however again project a little) and at the ends three bays curving forward.

While working on the Assembly Rooms between 1806-1811, the Greenway firm continued to follow the traditional builders' practice of buying partly finished houses in Clifton which they then completed and sold; but with the outbreak of war with France in 1809, and the ensuing slump, the Greenways, like many other builders, floundered and were declared bankrupt.

Before the bankruptcy, Greenway had contracted with Colonel Doolan to finish No.34 Cornwallis Crescent at a price of 1,300 guineas; after the bancruptcy Greenway claimed that Doolan had agreed to pay an additional £250 for the unfinished shell of the house, but he had no documents to prove it. Some time later Greenway produced a contract with an endorsement witnessed by a local solicitor collaborating the architect's statement. Doolan and the lawyer both refuted the document and Greenway was arrested on a charge of forgery.[5]

He was tried at the Bristol Assizes in March 1812; he pleaded guilty and was sentenced to death, but this was commuted to transportation for 14 years, probably due to some powerful family connections and to the fact that Greenway had been trying to help his creditors rather than make any personal profit.[6] Meanwhile another architect, Joseph Kay, completed the Assembly Rooms.

Greenway reached Sydney on 7 February 1814 in the convict ship *General Hewitt*, and was at once employed by Governor Macquarie in reporting on Government buildings then nearing completion; it is thought that Admiral Phillip, in retirement in Bath, recommended

Greenway – hence the speed of his appointment. Greenway was sharply critical of both the design and structure of many of the buildings he saw in Sydney and he was not hesitant in voicing his opinions.

In March 1816 Macquarie appointed him Civil Architect at a salary of 3s. a day, and encouraged him to develop plans for the improvement of Sydney. Understandably, perhaps, Greenway went over-the-top and produced a wild extravaganza of ideas for new forts, lighthouses, court houses, churches, a new Government House (based on Thornbury Castle, Avon), a circular wharf and even a bridge over the harbour to the North Shore with a lofty central span to allow tall-masted ships to pass under. He proposed to group round a focal circus (at the present Town Hall site) a cathedral, colleges, residences and a town hall; Hyde Park he

The Parramatta Road out of Sydney, engraved in 1829 by John Carmichael, showing Greenway's Gothic toll-house.

selected as the centre for the city's main administrative buildings, while the law courts were to occupy the site on which St James' Church now stands, and to be connected with the Convict Barrack by means of a Doric colonnade.[7]

The first building Greenway actually completed was a far more modest affair altogether; it has survived to become the oldest dwelling in Sydney and is preserved by the National Parks and Wildlife Service – Cadman's Cottage. The two storey building was built as the Coxswain's Barrack, and later occupied by John Cadman (1817-1827 Assistant Government Coxswain).[8]

Between 1816 and 1820 Greenway planned and superintended the erection of a number of important public buildings on which his reputation as the 'father of Australian architecture' now stands; these included Macquarie Lighthouse (completed in 1818), the Convict Barrack in Queen's Square, Sydney (1819), St Matthew's Church, Windsor (1820), and St Luke's Church, Liverpool (1820).

In 1817 the British Government sent out a Commissioner to investigate the goings-on in the colony, John Thomas Bigge; amongst many other things he was concerned by the flashy architecture and condemned it as 'too grand for an infant colony.'[9] Work was stopped instantly on Greenway's cathedral – despite the fact that Governor Macquarie had laid the foundation stone at a civic ceremony; and Bigge ordered Greenway, through the Governor, to convert his half-built courthouse into a church, now St James', and the adjoining schoolhouse into a court.

One of Greenway's most successful private commissions was the mansion he built at Point Eliza, now Piper Point, for John Piper, the Naval Officer in charge of Customs and water police; the house rivalled Government House in grandeur, with a domed ballroom, music rooms, salons and, lining the waterfront, a row of brass cannon with which Piper saluted his arriving guests.[10]

Few of Greenway's other grandiose schemes came to fruition; his work is best represented by St James' Church and the Government House stables. In 1821 Greenway, by then a free man, quarrelled with Macquarie by suddenly demanding £11,000 as fees for work he had done during the time he had worked for the Government on a salary. In the same year Macquarie was succeeded as Governor by Sir Thomas Brisbane; Macquarie wrote to Brisbane condemning Greenway's ingratitude and Greenway's numerous rivals were only too pleased to add fuel to the fire. In 1822 Greenway was dismissed.

From then on Greenway did no work of importance; he continued to pester the administration publicly and incessantly for his fees from a small farm, near Tarro railway station, in the Newcastle district, which Macquarie had granted him in 1821. He had married in or about 1804 a woman whose Christian name was Mary, but whose identity has not otherwise been established; she and several children voyaged to Sydney in 1814, and she died in 1832. The date and cause of Francis' death and the place of his burial are unknown, but the burial service was read over his body by the schoolmaster at Morpeth on 26 September 1837.[11]

The Australian artist and architect W.Hardy Wilson wrote of Greenway that 'with the barest means and economy in execution he produced architecture that has never been excelled in any land, giving the simplest structures a monumental scale, beautiful proportions and delightfully textured walls'.[12]

$10 bill, with a portrait of Francis Greenway and images of several of his most successful buildings. (By courtesy of the Reserve Bank of Australia)

The Tolpuddle Martyrs:

The 'Nobs of Old England' of shameful renown
Are striving to crush the poor man to the ground,
They'll beat down their wages and starve them complete
And make them work hard for Eight Shillings a week.[1]

Following the Swing riots of 1830 – the rick-burning, machine-breaking and threatening letters – the southern counties, as far west as Wiltshire, Dorset and the eastern fringes of Somerset were particularly sensitive to the mood of the agricultural workers. The magistrates, most of whom were also landowners, were determined that nothing like that should happen again. In some places the riots, though severely quelled, had had the desired effect and sympathetic farmers had slightly raised their men's wages, but this was not the case in the little village of Tolpuddle, just eight miles east of Dorchester.

The local Methodist preacher, George Loveless, a farm labourer himself, determined to try and improve the lot of his fellows and in 1832, at a village meeting, he successfully persuaded the masters, the farmers, to agree to raise the level of wages to equal those of others in the district. But the farmers did not keep their word and after another meeting at County Hall, Dorchester, they actually reduced wages from eight shillings a week to seven, and then to six[2].

The labouring men consulted together what to do; they knew that 'it was impossible to live honestly on such scanty means'[3], but they realised that to appeal again to the employers or magistrates would be in vain. Towards the end of October 1833, shortly after a visit from two members of a 'trade society', Loveless organised a meeting of about 40 local labourers at Thomas Standfield's cottage in the village, with the aim of forming a 'friendly society'. The rules and regulations were discussed in depth and it was resolved to start a Friendly Society of Agricultural Labourers in Tolpuddle, which would in due course be incorporated into the framework of the Grand National Consolidated Trades Union.

The Society was formed, and as such was perfectly legal; many of the village labourers joined and as membership expanded the news spread. On 9 December 1833 Edward Legg, a labourer, turned up for his initiation to be admitted[4]; it was the detail of this initiation which later led to the conviction of the 'Martyrs' – because although such 'societies' and unions were legal, oaths to secrecy were not.

Nothing particular occured until 21 February 1834, when out of the blue a bill-sticker toured the district posting up placards threatening transportation to any man who 'shall administer, or be present at, or consenting to the administering or taking any Unlawful Oath'; George Loveless, on his way to work, found a copy, read it and put it in his pocket. Just a couple of days later, the parish constable arrested him and the other members of the Friendly Society committee and marched them off to face the magistrates in Dorchester; the poster still in Loveless' pocket provided the proof that he was aware of the seriousness of his crime. Edward Legg was present at the initial interrogation and identified Loveless and Co as the leaders; they were immediately imprisoned to await trial at the forthcoming assizes. Loveless recorded:[5]

> As soon as we got within the prison doors, our clothes were stripped off and searched....After our heads were shorn, we were locked up together in a small room......I had never seen the inside of a gaol before, but now I began to feel it – disagreeable company, close confinement, bad bread, and what was worse, hard and cold lodging – a small straw bed on the flags, or else an iron bedstead – 'and this', said I to my companions, 'is our fare for striving to live honest.'

The magistrate, James Frampton, sought the advice of no less than the Home Secretary, Lord Melbourne, to whom he sent full details of the case; and in turn Melbourne sought the opinion of the Law Officers to ensure the swift and decisive carriage of justice.

On Monday morning, 17 March, the trial began; George and James Loveless (brothers), Thomas Standfield (the Lovelesses' brother-in-law) and his eldest son John, James Brine and James Hammett were brought up from their dingy cells beneath County Hall to face the judge – Mr Baron Williams. They were charged with administering 'a certain unlawful oath and engagement, purporting to bind the person taking the same, not to inform or give evidence against any associate or other person charged with any unlawful combination...'[6] The prosecution was on sure ground and quickly established the facts of the case with Edward Legg and another 'member of the secret society', John Lock, as witnesses, although under cross-examination both men testified to the good character of the accused.

The Counsel for the Defence argued that:[7]

> The poor man has as much right to protect the property he has in his labour as the rich man has to protect his accumulations of wealth. There has long ceased to be any restrictions on masters combining to reduce the rate of wages, or upon workmen to raise them.

AUSTRALIA BOUND

The judge inquired if the prisoners had anything to say, and Loveless instantly forwarded the following short statement, in writing:[8]

> My Lord, if we have violated any law, it was not done intentionally: we have injured no man's reputation, character, person, or property: we were uniting together to preserve ourselves, our wives, and our children, from utter degradation and starvation. We challenge any man to prove that we have acted, or intend to act, different from the above statement.

But the verdict was guilty and on the following day, the six men faced the judge again to hear their sentences. The Times reported Judge Williams' words:[9]

> Prisoners at the bar....I observed upon the trial, and in your defence, or in the defence of one of you that there is a statement that you meant no harm against any person, and that your intention was altogether without offence.
> Of the intentions of men it is impossible for man to judge – it is known only to each person and no other person can judge but by the conduct of the parties. But....there are cases in which, whatever may be the intention of the parties, the effect....upon the public security is of such a nature that the safety of that public does require a penal example to be made....
> I feel I have no discretion in a case of this sort....and accordingly the sentence is that you and each of you be transported to such places beyond the seas as his Majesty's Council in their discretion shall see fit for the term of seven years.

No sooner had the sentence been passed than Loveless scribbled in pencil a poem which was to become the rallying cry of the unions; he tossed the paper to the crowds as he and his colleagues were led from the prisoners' box:

> God is our guide! From field, from wave,
> From plough, from anvil and from loom,
> We come, our country's rights to save,
> And speak a tyrant faction's doom:
> We raise the watchword Liberty;
> We will, we will, we will be free!

God is our guide! No swords we draw.
We kindle not war's battle fires:
By reason, union, justice, law,
We claim the birthright of our sires:
We raise the watchword Liberty:
We will, we will, we will be free!

The convicted felons were manacled and escorted back to Dorchester Gaol. Loveless was taken ill with a severe fever or bronchitis – he claimed due to the foul conditions in the cells at County Hall, and for this reason he remained behind whilst the other were carted off to Portsmouth, chained 'like monkeys' to a coach. The Standfields, Brine and Hammett were imprisoned on the hulk *York*, while James Loveless was taken to the *Leviathan*. Just two days later they boarded the convict ship *Surrey* at Spithead and on 31 March set sail – initially to Plymouth to take on supplies and more convicts, and then on to New South Wales.

It was not until 5 April that Loveless was declared fit to travel; like the others he was chained to the outside of a coach to make the journey, and then re-chained aboard the *York*. Six weeks later he was taken to the convict ship *William Metcalfe* – its destination not New South Wales, but Van Dieman's Land. On the day before his departure he wrote to his wife:[10]

> I thank you, my dear wife, for that kind attention you have paid me, and you may safely rely upon it that as long as I live it will be my constant endeavour to return that kindness in every possible way, and hope to send to you as soon as we reach our place of destiny, and that I shall never forget the promises made at the altar; and though we may part a while I shall consider myself under the same obligation as though living in your immediate presence....Be satisfied, my dear Betsy, on my account. Depend on it, it will work together for good and we shall yet rejoice together.

While all this was going on, there was uproar around the country; the Trade Union newspaper *Pioneer* asked[11]:

> Will Britons see their honest labourers torn from home, and banished to a land of felony, the mark of infamy burnt on their brows; and honest husbandmen imprisoned among thieves and pick-pockets to cure them of their patriotism?

CAUTION.

WHEREAS it has been represented to us from several quarters, that mischievous and designing Persons have been for some time past, endeavouring to induce, and have induced, many Labourers in various Parishes in this County, to attend Meetings, and to enter into Illegal Societies or Unions, to which they bind themselves by unlawful oaths, administered secretly by Persons concealed, who artfully deceive the ignorant and unwary,—WE, the undersigned Justices think it our duty to give this PUBLIC NOTICE and CAUTION, that all Persons may know the danger they incur by entering into such Societies.

ANY PERSON who shall become a Member of such a Society, or take any Oath, or assent to any Test or Declaration not authorized by Law—

Any Person who shall administer, or be present at, or consenting to the administering or taking any Unlawful Oath, or who shall cause such Oath to be administered, although not actually present at the time—

Any Person who shall not reveal or discover any Illegal Oath which may have been administered, or any Illegal Act done or to be done—

Any Person who shall induce, or endeavour to persuade any other Person to become a Member of such Societies, WILL BECOME

Guilty of Felony,

AND BE LIABLE TO BE

Transported for Seven Years.

ANY PERSON who shall be compelled to take such an Oath, unless he shall declare the same within four days, together with the whole of what he shall know touching the same, will be liable to the same Penalty.

Any Person who shall directly or indirectly maintain correspondence or intercourse with such Society, will be deemed Guilty of an Unlawful Combination and Confederacy, and on Conviction before one Justice, on the Oath of one Witness, be liable to a Penalty of TWENTY POUNDS, or to be committed to the Common Gaol or House of Correction, for THREE CALENDAR MONTHS; or for every other offence committed after Conviction, be deemed Guilty of such Unlawful Combination and Confederacy, and on Conviction before one Justice, on the Oath of one Witness, be liable to a Penalty of TWENTY POUNDS, or to Commitment to the Common Gaol or House of Correction, FOR THREE CALENDAR MONTHS; or if proceeded against by Indictment may be

CONVICTED OF FELONY,

And Transported for SEVEN YEARS.

COUNTY OF DORSET,
Dorchester Division.

February 22d, 1834.

C. B. WOLLASTON,
JAMES FRAMPTON,
WILLIAM ENGLAND,
THOS. DADE,
JNO. MORTON COLSON,

HENRY FRAMPTON,
RICHD. TUCKER STEWARD
WILLIAM R. CHURCHILL,
AUGUSTUS FOSTER.

G. CLARK, PRINTER, CORNHILL, DORCHESTER.

The poster, printed in Dorchester, threatening transportation to those found guilty of joining illegal societies 'to which they bind themselves by unlawful oaths'; February 1834.

And a mass meeting, addressed by Robert Owen, the co-operative socialist leader, in London attracted 10,000 people. A petition was prepared for presentation to the King and other petitions from provincial towns, like Oxford, Cheltenham and Yeovil, bombarded parliament, pleading for clemency and questioning the unjustifiable severity of the sentences. By August 1834 an official 'London Dorchester Committee' had been set up to maintain the barrage of pressure and to agitate on behalf of the convicts' families. The magistrate, Frampton, continued his vindictive behaviour by refusing to grant parish relief to the dependants of the six men; Diana Standfield, with five children to support, was told: 'You shall suffer want. You shall have no mercy, because you ought to have known better than to have allowed such meetings to have been holden in your house'.[12] The unions quickly stepped in, organised a subscription scheme and sent a Mr Newman, a cabinet-maker from London, to Tolpuddle 'to convey money to the wives and families of the convicts'.

The climax of the campaign was a mass demonstration at Copenhagen Fields (north of King's Cross), London, on 21 April; a mammoth petition bearing something like 300,000 signatures was displayed on a waggon which led a huge procession through the streets of the city to the Home Office. Estimates of the numbers involved in the march vary from 20,000 to 200,000, but that and the fact that Lord Melbourne refused to accept the petition are unimportant compared to the cohesion and unity the event brought to the national trades union movement and the long-term effect on the fates of the Tolpuddle men.

On arrival in New South Wales John and Thomas Standfield, James Loveless, Brine and Hammett were each assigned to work. Brine for example was sent at first to the General Hospital in Sydney to work for James Mitchell, a surgeon; later he was transferred to a farm at Glindon, up the Hunter River – apparently he caught a steamboat to Newcastle and part way up the river and was then dropped off, with 'a small bed and blanket, a suit of 'new slops' and a shilling'[13] to make his own way the last 30 miles to the farm. The poor fellow was attacked by bush-rangers one night and robbed of everything and of course when at last he arrived at the farm his new employer refused to believe his story. Thomas Standfield was assigned as a shepherd and by chance his son, John, was posted to a farm only a few miles away – both near the Hunter River.

The *William Metcalfe* dropped anchor off Hobart Town on 4 September 1834. George Loveless's particulars were carefully recorded:[14]

Trade:	Ploughman
Height:	5ft 4½in.
Age:	37
Complexion:	brown
Head:	Small
Hair:	brown
Whiskers:	dark red
Visage:	small
Forehead:	low
Eyes:	dark hazel
Nose:	small
Mouth:	med.wide
Chin:	small dimpled
Remarks:	small scar on upper lip, scar on L.arm
Native place:	Nr.Dorset

Loveless was questioned at length by the assistant police magistrate, Thomas Mason, and a statement sent back to London together with a surprisingly radical note from Governor George Arthur[15]: 'If this man's statement is to be credited, it is evident that he and his companions have ignorantly become the victims of more artful men'.

Loveless had been destined to work in irons on the roads, but, it is said, the Governor intervened and put him to work on Domain Farm, a government establishment for the production of 'Vice-Regal and institutional vegetables and meat'.[16]

Meanwhile the cause of the Tolpuddle men had not been forgotten in London; Thomas Wakley M.P. presented 16 petitions to the House of Commons appealing for a total remission of the sentences passed and called for a full debate; he pleaded their cause in an emotive and powerful two-hour long speech, arguing amongst other things that the oaths to secrecy taken by members of the Orange Lodges, which included many noble lords, were 'exactly similar to that taken by the Dorchester labourers'. The new Home Secretary, Lord John Russell, was considerably more sympathetic than his predecessor – who had moved on to become Prime Minister. It was proposed that the wives and families of the convicts should be sent out to Australia to mitigate the sentences of their menfolk. Then on 12 June 1835, the Colonial Secretary wrote to the governors, of New South Wales and Van Dieman's Land, authorizing pardons to be granted to the men – but on condition that the Lovelesses remained in the colony and the others could only return home after serving two years. Pressure from Wakley continued and incredibly on 14 March 1836 Lord Russell, in answer to Wakley's persistant enquiry, announced that 'His Majesty had been pleased to grant a free pardon to the whole of the persons who had been convicted on the occasion to which the Honourable Member referred'.[17]

News of the various moves within the Home Office travelled slowly; the letters to the governors suggesting the family link-up, then conditional pardons and finally free pardons appeared contradictory, so that even after the correspondence had arrived, there was extraordinary delay in carrying out the instructions. By February 1836 George Loveless was more-or-less free – not able to return home, but at least not under penal servitude. He found employment on a farm at Glen Ayr, near Richmond. Although Governor Arthur received Loveless's pardon in July 1836, it was not until Loveless read an article, about the goings-on in London, in the local paper, the *Tasmanian*, in September, that he learnt that he really was free. He waited to see whether he would be informed officially, then at the end of the month he wrote to the newspaper[18]:

> I do not know whether Governor Arthur has received orders from home; I should like to know. If His Excellency has received intelligence to that effect, I hope he will have the goodness to communicate that knowledge to me before he leaves these shores.

Shortly after the publication of the letter, Loveless received his pardon and was told that he could have a free passage home on the *Elphinstone*. Wonderful news! but only a few months before he had been persuaded to write to his wife to encourage her to join him in Van Dieman's Land – 'It would be a dreadful thing for me to leave before I have heard from my wife, to know if she intends coming or not, for her to find, when she arrives in Hobart Town, I had gone to London'. The authorities did not like their arrangements being altered one little bit, but Loveless persuaded them to allow him to stay until he had heard from his wife, and then to return with a free passage.

Eventually Loveless received a letter from his wife explaining that she had decided not to make the journey, as she was aware of the agitation for the release and pardon of her husband and his friends; so at last he was able to start for home. On 28 January 1837 he boarded the *Eveline* as a steerage passenger, and a couple of days later she sailed for London.

The release of the other men in New South Wales was just as tardy and the delays compounded by bureaucratic ineptitude; summoned to leave their farms and be brought down to the barracks in Hyde Park, Sydney, at one stage James Brine was put on a boat for Norfolk Island and it was only his vigorous protestations that brought the bungle to the attention of the overseers. By the end of February 1837, the Standfields, James Loveless and Brine were safely in Sydney; Hammett had arrived by May. The five were sent off to work again for a time while arrangements were made to ship them home. The colonial government then paid out £25 per man to obtain a free passage for each of them on the *John Barry*, sailing from Sydney in September – Captain Robson, sympathetic to their case, had craftily managed to add an extra £5 to each fare so that the men could provide themselves with necessities for the voyage, and have something in their pockets when they arrived in England; oddly enough, and no one seems quite sure why, James Hammett was not on that boat home.

George Loveless, the first to get back, arrived in London on 13 June 1837 to a welcome by the London Dorchester Committee; he returned to his cottage in Tolpuddle and almost immediately set about writing his account of his experiences in *The Victims of Whiggery*, published in September that year.

On 16 March 1838, the *John Barry* docked in Plymouth, a plaque on the quayside marks the spot where James Loveless, James Brine, and Thomas and John Standfield stepped ashore. Plymouth trade unionists laid on the hospitality; the *Plymouth, Devonport and Stonehouse Herald* of 24 March reported[19]:

> ...These men on landing were received by members of the Trades Union in these towns, and treated, we learn, with much kindness and attention.
>
> We have been informed that the Captain and Officers of the *John Barry* speak in high terms of the behaviour of these men during the voyage...
>
> On Thursday evening a public meeting was held at the Mechanics Institute... A penny collection was made for them at

JAMES BRINE   THOMAS STANFIELD   JOHN STANFIELD
Aged 25   Aged 51   aged 25

GEORGE LOVELESS   JAMES LOVELESS
Aged 41   Aged 29

The returned and pardoned convicts, portrayed in Cleave's Penny Gazette, *12 May, 1838.*

the door. These men left Plymouth on the following day for their respective homes.

On the way back to Dorset they stopped over in Exeter for another welcoming event. Not to be outdone, the London Dorchester Committee then arranged the 'official' welcome in London.

103

Monday being the day appointed for the celebration of the liberation and return of the Dorchester labourers by a public procession through the metropolis and a dinner at White Conduit House, various members of the different working classes began to assemble as previously arranged on Kennington Common as early as 7 o'clock....

Before nine, however, several thousands of operatives all attired in their holiday clothing had arrived on the common....

About a quarter before ten a general huzza announced the arrival of the Dorchester labourers. They were in an open carriage drawn by four fine grey horses, and as they were drawn through the lines acknowledged the congratulations of the assembled thousands of their brother labourers by remaining uncovered and repeatedly bowing to all within view.[20]

At the celebration dinner, the Reverend Dr Wade thanked Almighty God for the return of the Dorchester labourers from beyond the seas

The Martyrs memorial gate at the Methodist Chapel, Tolpuddle.

and, proposing the first toast, Mr Wakely suggested that they should resolve that the labourers should be labourers no longer, 'let them make farmers of them all'.[21] Contributions were called for so that farms could be purchased.

The Farm Tribute accumulated sufficient funds for large deposits to be put down on the leaseholds of two farms in Essex; the men left Dorset in August 1838 for their new homes, supplied with the necessary capital by the London Dorchester Committee. But ex-convicts and radicals were no more popular in Essex than they would have been in Dorset, and in the 1840s the men and their families emigrated to Canada where they made a pact to keep the story of their past a secret, even from their younger children.

James Hammett returned to England in 1839; he did not go back to Dorset immediately, but joined the Lovelesses and Brines in Essex, together with his wife, Harriet, and family. However, by 1841 he was back in Tolpuddle, where he stayed for the rest of his life. He died in the Dorchester Workhouse in 1891.[22]

6   PUSH ME - PULL YOU

It is no mere coincidence that a glance at the population statistics of rural parishes throughout the South West during the nineteenth century reveals an almost constant trend; generally the population reached a peak in the 1840s or 1850s, and then, across the board, sunk into a decline, whilst at the same time the populations of the counties as wholes increased more rapidly than ever before. The peak for these rural parishes, whatever its level, was often not to be reached again until the post-war (1939-45) population boom, when village life became a desirable alternative to suburbia and accessible through the ubiquitous motor car. There is rarely a simple answer to such dramatic swings in the pendulum of population figures, and many factors contributed to bring about these changes.

Many of those who left the countryside headed for nearby towns and developing industrial centres, ports, military establishments and seaside resorts – Bristol and Bath attracted many seeking employment in service; Weston-super-Mare needed builders and craftsmen, and waitresses and chambermaids to cater for the recent influx of summer visitors; Portland wanted labourers and craftsmen to build new fortifications; the success of the Clarks' shoemaking venture in Street (Somerset) drew labourers from the neighbourhood to expand that village to a prosperous and paternalistic model industrial town. The coming of the railways offered opportunities to work in the new 'transport' towns like Swindon, and expanded the horizons of all who could watch the thundering engines roaring towards London or Birmingham. The industrial connurbations of the Midlands and the North both competed with and defeated the traditional West Country craftsmen, and then having brought about the decline, they sucked the skilled workers, the adventurous and the ambitious to join them, leaving the die-hard plodders to fight an impossible rearguard action in their wake.

In 1851, for example, throughout Wiltshire, parishes cited emigration as the cause of their declining populations – Calne, Great and Little Cheverell, Chippenham, Devizes, Eisey, Hardenhuish, Heytesbury, Hindon, West Knoyle, Lacock, Melksham and Westbury;[1] some attributed it to the decline in the wool trade, others to the depression in agriculture, and certainly low wages were another factor. In Cornwall the parishes of Breage and Germoe lost 27 per cent of their populations between 1841-51, and Perranzabuloe lost 22 per cent between 1871-81. In Dorset, Somerset and Devon the story was the same. A proportion of these emigrants, the younger ones and the most daring, made the startling decision to go, not to Taunton or Salisbury, or Exeter, or even London, but to head for a new life in a new world – America, Canada, Australia or New Zealand.

For us, now, it is very difficult to imagine what could start such a common movement of migration; in order to understand the mood of the people in the countryside in the nineteenth century, contemporary sources help to recreate the atmosphere: William Cobbett, travelling down the valley of the Wiltshire Avon in the 1820s observed the countryside during its most depressed phase; he raved at a system which forced the farm labourers to work for starvation wages whilst producing an abundance of food:[2]

> What injustice, what a hellish system it must be, to make those who raise it skin and bone and nakedness, while the food and drink and wool are almost all carried away to be heaped on the fund-holders, pensioners, soldiers, dead-weight, and the other swarms of tax-eaters! If such an operation do not need putting an end to, then the devil himself is a saint.

Cobbett was appalled at the antics of the 'Emigration Committee' which wanted to 'transport those who raise this food, because they want to eat enough of it to keep them alive'.[3] 'Dogs and hogs and horses' he wrote, 'are treated with more civility; and as to food and lodging, how gladly would the labourers change with them!'[4]

Part of the problem was the vicious Speenhamland system of public relief which paid part of the labourer's miserable wages out of the poor rates; it encouraged the farmers and landowners to lay off men after the harvest, to leave them to survive as best they could through the winter months. Cobbett also observed that most of the old common lands had, by now, been enclosed – in the past cottagers and labourers alike had been able to keep a cow or some sheep for themselves, and to tend a

107

Living conditions for agricultural workers in England were appalling: overcrowded, damp and cold; and the labourers lived on a near-starvation diet.

vegetable patch; such bonuses had become rare offerings from only the best of landlords.

Cobbett saw the effects of the declining cloth industry: in Heytesbury (Wiltshire) he met men and boys 'who had come all the way from Bradford [on-Avon], about 12 miles, in order to get nuts. These people were men and boys that had been employed in the cloth factories at Bradford and about Bradford'.[5] And in Frome he was welcomed into the town by the sight of 'between two and three hundred weavers, men and boys, cracking stones, moving earth and doing other sorts of work, towards making a fine road into the town....The parish pay, which they now get...is 2s6d a week for a man, 2s for his wife, 1s3d for each child under eight years of age, 3d a week, in addition, to each child above eight, who can go to work; and, if the children above eight years old, whether girls or boys, do not go to work upon the road, they have nothing!'[6]

The level of wages was cited by all commentators as desperately low; Sir Frederick Morton Eden who visited Dorset in the 1790s to report on *The State of the Poor*, found that farm labourers at Blandford received 6s or 7s a week. He described the domestic economy of one family – a labourer aged 52, one daughter aged 18 who kept house for him (his wife had died shortly before Eden's visit), another daughter of 8 and two sons aged 6 and 3; the man earned six shillings a week in winter, seven shillings a week in summer and slightly more during the harvest; the children earned nothing; the parish paid their house rent and for clothing they relied on gifts from neighbours. Their food consisted of:

Breakfast: Tea or bread and cheese
Dinner and Supper: Bread and cheese, or potatoes, sometimes mashed with fat from broth, and sometimes with salt alone. Bullock's cheek is generally bought every week to make broth. Treacle is used to sweeten tea instead of sugar. Very little milk or beer is used.[8]

In the 1850s a typical weekly shopping list for an agricultural labourer and his family in Somerset was as follows:[9]

Bread 6d per 4lb loaf	5 loaves	2s6d
Potatoes 6d per peck	3 pecks	1s6d
Bacon 7d per lb	½ lb	3½d
Tea 4d per ounce	½ lb	1d
Soap 6d per lb	½ lb	3d
Candles 6d per lb	½ lb	1½d
Coal 10d per cwt	½ cwt	5d
Turf 8d per cwt	¼ cwt	1d
House rent 1s6d per week		1s6d
	Total	6s9½d

and that left precious little over for any other necessities – boots, clothes, medicine – let alone the occasional 'luxury'.

An anonymous record of life in Somerset in the 1840s described farm workers reduced to eating horse beans[10]; and even towards the end of the century Richard Jefferies pointed out his observation of the labourer that:[11]

His food may perhaps have something to do with the deadened slowness which seems to pervade everthing de does – there seems a lack of vitality about him. It consists chiefly of bread and cheese, with bacon twice or thrice a week varied with onions....

The worst fate of all, for the destitute, was to end their days in the workhouse. Here inmates earn their keep by breaking stones.

In the Channel Islands, the 'Hungry Forties' (1840s) saw wages pegged at two shillings a day, while the price of bread was rising weekly; in February 1847 the States of Jersey decided to offer loaves at a special price of 4 sous as against the normal price of 5 sous; however with unemployment rising and the price of flour increasing the States then discontinued their cheaper loaves. There was a riot in St Helier as a great gang of hungry workers marched to the town mill.[12]

If the food was bad, housing conditions were even worse; at Edington Burtle near Bridgwater (Somerset) in 1870:[13]

John Holly lives in half an old dilapidated cottage on the moor (Sedgemoor). Water comes up to the door in floods, and we had to jump two peat ditches to get there. They have a plank, but that had been removed. It has two rooms, one above and one below; in it live a father, mother, two big sons, daughter aged 19, with a child. The mother was out at work. A girl of 9 was kept at home to look after the baby.

George Mitchell, reporting to the Royal Commission on the Housing of the Working Classes in 1884, described a cottage in Wiveliscombe (Somerset) that he had visited with Mr Clifford of *The Times*:[14]

In one house I found that there were seven children with the mother and father in one room upstairs. In three or four places in the thatched roof great wisps of straw were pushed up to keep the rain out. It was wet while Mr Clifford and I were there, and the rain was pouring down on the bedroom floor and saturating the floor below. While we were there the mother was out at work washing; and those seven children were without anybody to look after them besides themselves, and they were in a state of starvation.

Q. What was the husband? A farm labourer.
Q. What wages had he? Eight shillings a week when he could get work.

Of course there were landlords who made sure that their staff were well cared for; many of the largest landowners initiated schemes to help the labourers on their estates; in Somerset, for example, Sir Alexander Hood, Lord Taunton, Sir Thomas Acland and Sir Arthur Elton each built model cottages for their tenants[15] – but such philanthropists were in a minority.

On the land, the recession in agriculture at the end of the Napoleonic Wars exacerbated an already miserable situation. By 1815 13 per cent of the total population of Dorset was receiving parish relief. By 1830 the appalling low wages, bad conditions and long hours of work stirred even the normally passive Dorset labourers to protest and many joined the widespread rioting, rick burning and machine breaking which swept through southern England during the Autumn of that year – the notorious 'Captain Swing' riots.[16] As if low wages were not enough to contend with, innovative farmers were now trying to introduce new-fangled machines – 'Under the old system, a dozen men worked all winter through, hammering away with their flails in the barns. Now the threshing machine arrives, and the ricks are threshed in a few days'.[17] We can hardly be surprised that the labourers felt threatened.

Bread of dependance never would be sweet
Even were it mine, which it is not, to eat:
With God's good blessing on me I will go,
And manly independance I will show.
There is no room in this o'ercrowded land
For men to rise, nay, hardly room to stand;
Men packed and jostled are, too tight, too close
And hence grow selfish, savage and morose.
No, I will seek a wider scope and sphere,
Than industry and genius can find here –
Will forfeit luxury and ease, and press
My way into the distant wilderness.[18]

Where did all these wandering emigrants go? The majority moved to improved opportunities within this country – as described above; of the 13 million or so that decided to go abroad between 1815 and 1895, the United States of America was by far the most popular choice, followed by Canada; Australia and New Zealand were third on the list – and a pretty poor third at that:[19]

Destination of Emigrants from U.K.

Year	Canada	USA	Australia/NZ	Elsewhere/S.Africa
1821	12,995	4,958	320	384
1831	58,067	23,418	1,561	114
1841	38,164	45,017	32,625	2,786
1851	42,605	267,357	21,532	4,472
1861	12,707	49,764	23,738	5,561
1871	32,671	198,843	12,227	8,694
1881	34,561	307,973	24,093	25,887
1891	33,752	252,016	19,957	28,818

Apart from the obvious fact that Canada and America were much closer, they also had a long-established history of successful immigration; Australia, on the other hand, carried the stigma of being a convict colony, and was at the furthest remove possible.

If anything, the relative newness of Australia as a possible destination for emigrants acted as a positive advantage; here was a vast, if unknown, country refreshingly free of many of the more oppressive Victorian values, where even convicts could emerge and make good. There was an optimism about this new world, reflected in the hope of Charles Dickens' Wilkins Micawber that something would 'turn up' there.[20]

The opportunities promised attracted those with a little capital; second or third sons, without the inheritance of the family farm, were destined, back home, for the church or the army. In Australia they stood a good chance of acquiring some land, and farming for themselves. In the early years, squatters just headed off into the bush with a flock of sheep and maybe a couple of convict servants – if they found a good 'run' and all went well, they could find themselves grazing a couple of thousand acres within a few years.[21]

Australia was crying out for farm labourers; wages were far higher than in England, as much as 10 shillings a day in Melbourne in the 1860s[22]; at that rate plain and simple day labourers could reckon to work for a couple of years to save up some capital, and then they, too, could launch into a farm of their own. Builder's labourers and pick and shovel men received 7 shillings and 6 shillings respectively per day. The *Melbourne Argus* reported that:[23]

so much of the land has been taken up by men who in former years were farm labourers themselves, and so much more is likely to be entered upon under the new act which was passed last week, establishing free selection over the whole of the colony, that a steadily growing demand for agricultural labour is likely to exist for years to come.

The example of Jacob Baker, a labourer from the tiny hamlet of Hodson, south of Swindon (Wiltshire), with nine children and no regular work through the winter months, graphically contrasts his lot in England with that in Australia: in the *Devizes Gazette* of Valentines Day, 1850, he asked:[24]

How would you like to sit down with your wife and young children four days in the week to not half bread and potatoes enough, and the other three days upon not half enough boiled swedes, and but little fire to cook them with?

A cartoon by John Leech titled 'Here and there, or Emigration a remedy', *published in* Punch, *1848.*

115

The following year, 1851, he and his family emigrated to South Australia, where he found no shortage of work and within a couple of years was writing home:[25]

> Poor pipel in Hodson do not know what good living is. We have got a goint of fresh meet on our tabel everey day, and littel Bill says I want to give Tom Weston some. [Little Bill was six years old, and Tom Weston was a chum of his in Hodson]. We do not put tea in the pot with a tea-spuoan, but with a hand!....This is the contrey, my boys....'

There certainly was no lack of work in Australia for those willing to roll up their sleeves and get on with it and, unlike home, they would be well rewarded.

The young country was as desperate as the young men (and indeed the older ones) to attract women – both to equalise the proportions between the sexes and to provide domestic help; a cook or laundress could command a salary of £30-40 per year, plus board and lodging, a parlour maid got £30, and a general servant £25-30. Female immigrants were snapped up, almost before they had time to get off the boat:

> On Friday last it was notified that 23 young girls who had just arrived by the *Charlotte Gladstone* would be open to engagement at 11 o'clock in the morning at the Immigration Depot in this city [Melbourne]. Five minutes sufficed to procure situations for the whole of them at wages averaging from £20 to £30 per annum....300 female immigrants of the class above referred to could have met with immediate engagements, if such a number had been forthcoming.[26]

Apart from attracting young workers, Australia was also recommended to those on low fixed incomes – rates and taxes were considerably lower than in England.[27]

Australia's healthy climate was advertised as another attraction; there emigrants could escape the cold and fog of England; mortality rates in Hobart Town were way below those of Europe. Promoting the antipodes in Thomas Braim's tome *New Homes..*, Dr Bird wrote:[28]

> But the climate par excellence of these colonies is that of Moreton Bay and its neighbourhood, in Queensland, not far from the

southern limit of the tropics. Here the average winter temperature on the coast is 62°or 63°, warmer even than Madeira – an air soft and soothing, without being relaxing, and sunny brilliant weather.

The climate, he reckoned, was 'ideal for invalids'.

But the greatest influence on Australia as a popular destination for

'Emigration in search of a husband', *a cartoon of 1833; the porter asks: 'What are you going to Sidney for, pray ma'am. And the large lady replies: 'Vy they says as how theres lots of good husbands to be had cheap whereas the brutes in England can't see no charms in a woman unles she's got plenty of money to keep 'em in idleness'.*

emigrants was undoubtedly the offer of free passages – assisted emigration. Throughout the South West newspapers and posters blasted the news that free passages were available, particularly to those with specific skills – mechanics, carpenters, masons and handicraftsmen, and to single women.

The price of the fare to Australia given in Cassell's *Emigration Handbook* of 1852 was £15 for a berth in the steerage, with basic provisions; a cabin passenger could expect to pay up to £90. Children under 14 years old paid half fare, and infants under one year were carried free of charge. £15 was far more than a labourer could ever hope to save from his weekly wage, and yet Australia was crying out for labourers whilst Poor Law commissioners in the South West were battling against unemployment and too many mouths to feed.

It was Edward Gibbon Wakefield who initially promoted the idea of systematic emigration assisted by the government. He recognised that Australia needed capital, managerial skill and labour, but that there was a tendency in the colony for a few capitalists to acquire, by grant, more land than they could use and for labourers to become subsistence farmers rather than working for employers. So why not sell land rather than grant it? And then use the revenue to assist emigration.[29] In 1831, the Colonial Office agreed to try the 'Wakefield System' to develop the settlement of South Australia; land was offered for sale at a minimum price of 12 shillings per acre and the assisted emigrants were embarked at Plymouth.

In 1835 a new plan was devised to cater more specifically for the precise needs of settlers already in Australia – the Bounty System enabled farmers, land owners and merchants in Australia to categorise the workers they required and to purchase 'bounty orders' for them; agents in England would then select appropriate emigrants and arrange their passage. On arrival in Australia the emigrants were assured of a job, and a refund on the bounty order could be obtained.[30]

In Totnes (Devon) in 1841, an agent for the Australian Agricultural Company, Mr Bentall, simply selected shepherds and labourers from the area and shipped them out – the list included Thomas Lavers, his wife and three children; Richard Martin with his wife and child; John Edwards, his wife and four children; Philip Pillage, John Tottel and Richard Cross, all single men; George Evans and John Jarvis who, it was noted, were engaged to be married but sailed single. Two men, John Martin and John Germon, clearly got cold feet and 'absconded in

England'; and one William Birch's daughter refused to go so the family remained in England. Those that did go arrived safely at Port Jackson in the ship *Ganges* on 23 June 1842.[31]

In 1840 the Colonial Land and Emigration Commission was established as a sub-section of the Colonial Office; initially four ports, London, Liverpool, Southampton and Plymouth, were nominated for the despatch of government sponsored emigrants, but these were later reduced to two – just London and Plymouth. In Plymouth a Government Emigration Agent was appointed, to inspect emigrant vessels, to check their accomodation, victualling and general seaworthiness; and a Commissioners Despatching Agent was responsible for procurring supplies for emigrants, overseeing their accomodation in Plymouth and for arranging for the emigrants to be rowed out to the vessels moored in the Sound or Cattewater.

A network of semi-official selecting agents throughout the South West emerged; it was their job to advertise for potential emigrants and make an initial selection – assisted emigrants, they were instructed, should be

> sober, industrious, and of good moral character;....They must also be in good health, free from all bodily and mental defects, and the adults must be in all respects capable of labour and going out to work for wages.[32]

The agents then passed the list of names on to the Government Emigration Agent. The emigrants who sailed in the ship *Orleana* in 1842 were selected by agents dotted throughout the south-western counties:[33]

Bradford-on-Avon	James Chant
"	R.P.Hyatt
Taunton	A.A.Mullett
Exeter	George Pye
Launceston	John Geake
Plymouth	John Alger
"	James Wilcocks
Liskeard	George Jennings
Truro	Isaac Latimer
Falmouth	A.B.Duckham
Redruth	Two doors above the shoemarket

James Wilcocks was particularly active in Plymouth; the previous year he had published a pamphlet promoting *Emigration its Necessity and Advantages*, a copy of which he presented to the Devon and Exeter Institution, where it has remained to this day. In 1848 he became the first permanently appointed Commissioners Despatching Agent in Plymouth. Business was booming for emigration agents; by 1850 six agents, other than Wilcocks, were listed under Plymouth in White's Directory:[34]

Collier and Son, Southside Street
Foulds Wm. Hy., 6 Marine Place
Fox Sons and Co., Hoegate Street
Johnson S.C., The Parade
Luscombe, Driscoll and Co., Vauxhall Street
Walker J., Parade Wharf

In 1849 a total of 130 emigrant ships sailed from Plymouth carrying 15,895 passengers; of which 109 ships with 14,118 passengers went to Australia; just 10 ships with 1,171 passengers to Canada; and the rest to the Cape, United States, Port Natal and San Francisco.[35] By 1857 Plymouth boasted an 'Emigrants' Home':

a commodious building, situate at the Baltic Wharf, Commercial Road...capable of affording shelter and a temporary home for no less than 700 emigrants, whilst waiting for the vessel destined to bear them to a distant land.[36]

and a 'Ladies' Female Emigrant Society' at No.3 Commercial Road, under the 'immediate patronage' of the Countess of Mount Edgcumbe, the Countess of Morley, and other ladies of distinction; its object was to 'administer instruction and advice to the emigrants during their stay...and to prepare and distribute employment amongst them to wile away their time during their long and tedious voyage'.[37]

In spite of the work of the Emigration agents and their advertisments, and the facilities available, it was not always easy to get the message through to the ordinary labourers they hoped to attract. Local enthusiasts for emigration, often the gentry or clergy, played a vital role in priming the pump; Sidney Herbert, at Wilton House (Wiltshire), helped a number of labourers and their families from that estate to emigrate in 1850 – one George Bennett, whose sister was married to Joseph Blake, a gardener at Wilton, encouraged the Blakes to come out and join him; they did, on the emigrant ship *Marion*, which was wrecked off the coast of South Australia, but the passengers survived.[38] Earl Bruce, later 2nd Marquis of Ailesbury, founded the Wiltshire Emigration Association in 1849, and over a period of only three years it arranged the emigration of more than 250 Wiltshire people, farm labourers and their wives and children, to South Australia and Victoria.[39]

In addition to government sponsored emigrants and those informed and encouraged by individuals, others were financed by their local parishes or churches, largely as the most expedient way of reducing their charge on the poor rate. Between 1836 and 1841, for example, the Reverend John West of Chettle (Dorset) arranged to send out to New South Wales a number of paupers from the Tisbury Union workhouse, some of them from the neighbouring villages of Donhead St Mary and Donhead St Michael.[40] A few years later, in 1849, the Reverend S.G.Osborne supervised the emigration of 18 people from Maiden Newton (Dorset) and 135 from Blandford (Dorset); they sailed from Plymouth on the *Lady Peel* and the local paper reported that:[41]

> Through the kind exertions of that gentleman and his friends these poor people were all well provided with clothing and necessities and each had a substantial locked chest for the security of his worldly goods....Mr Osborne remained with his charge until the pilot left the ship.

In 1843 the rate payers of the parish of Collingbourne Ducis (Wiltshire) were called to a meeting on 15 December to 'consider whether any and what sum or sums of money, not exceeding half the average yearly poor-rate...shall be raised or borrowed as a fund for defraying the expenses of the Emigration of poor persons having settlements in this parish, and being willing to emigrate'.[42] It was agreed that £65 should be borrowed, to be repaid over the following five years, to meet the costs of the following emigrants:

John Waters, 37 years old, a labourer, his wife Mary (38) also a labourer, and their children, James (15) a shepherd, Ann (10), Charlotte (8), Emma (6) and Martha (3); Thomas Waters (33) labourer, his wife Sarah (35) labourer, and children Robert (6) and George (3); Obadiah Lewis (22) a labourer, and his wife Martha (30) a cook; and Henry Wadham (22) a shepherd.[43]

AUSTRALIA BOUND

The expenses were meticulously listed:[44]

	£	s	d
To Carter and Bonus Emigration Agents			
London for head money for 9 persons	9	0	0
To ditto for 7 children under 14 years	3	10	0
To Mr Waters of Ludgershall as per contract			
for taking the emigrants to Deptford	5	0	0
To ditto for 16 breakfasts & suppers at			
Andover Station		18	0
for fares by train	5	12	0
for 5½cwt extra luggage		16	6
for waggon from London to Deptford		18	6
for Articles of Clothing as per bill	1	17	0
for 4 days keep for the party	2	0	0
Advanced on John Waters Goods	1	10	0
To Mr Davis for Clothing as per Bill	7	19	7
Miss Sheppard ditto	3	18	3
Mr Allen ditto	15	16	11
Mrs Gulliver to several people for			
making Changes for the Emigrants	2	5	2
Mrs Green for conveying the Emigrants			
to Andover Station	1	5	0
	62	6	11

Similarly at Chard (Somerset) Arthur Hull, diarist, assistant overseer and collector of rates, recorded that on the 21 October 1848 he 'Put up Notice of Emigration Eve'; on 27 October: 'I at Emigration Vestry'; and on 16 November: 'At Mr Eames Eve. about sending Wm. Gaylard's family to Australia'. On 9 December he made the general observation: 'Many people are going to Australia' and the following April he helped to fit out William Gaylard, his wife and six children and accompanied them to Plymouth to see them aboard the *Victoria* bound for Sydney.[45]

Self-financed or assisted, 'bounty' or Wakefield, emigration certainly did not appeal to everyone; it is quite understandable that the young tended to be more attracted than the old, single men particularly and young families looking for advancement. To try and analyse these

Poster advertising free passages to Australia, printed in Truro (Cornwall), 1840. (By courtesy of the Royal Institution of Cornwall) generalisations more precisely for West Country emigrants, the following statistics have been taken from the immigration lists of all those who arrived at Moreton Bay between January 1857 and September 1858 from Cornwall, Devon, Somerset and Dorset[46]; they were all assisted immigrants and on arrival were asked to give their name, age, calling, native place and country, parents' names and, if alive, their residence, religious denomination, reading and writing skill, existence of relatives in the colony and state of health. Out of a total of 2614 immigrants arriving on eight vessels during the period, 493 (19 per cent) were from those four counties. On one ship, the *Ascendant*, which arrived in the Bay on 24 June 1858, 37 per cent of the passengers were of West Country origin.

280 (57 per cent) of the West Country immigrants were male; and of those, 137 (49 per cent) were aged between 16 and 25:

Female	*Ages*	*Male*
1	51+	1
4	46-50	5
9	41-45	8
10	36-40	20
12	31-35	13
22	26-30	30
41	21-25	76
33	16-20	61
19	11-15	15
22	06-10	17
40	01-05	34

Just 35 of the females aged 14 and over were single – and of them, 12 were travelling with their parents; 123 of the males over 14 were single, and only 14 of them were with their families.

Nearly 70 per cent of the men (aged 14+) gave their occupation as 'labourer'; of the rest four were gardeners, three wheelwrights, two shepherds, two blacksmiths and two masons, and one of each of the following: carpenter, ploughman, carter, groom, brickmaker, bricklayer, excavator, wool comber and domestic servant. Of the 38 women who stated an occupation (the single women and widows with families – the remainder would, today, be classified as 'housewives', although almost certainly most of them went on to take up some sort of employment), 36 were domestic servants; the exceptions were a clothier and a dairymaid; it is also interesting to note that 24 of them had relatives in the colony – variously stated: 'aunt in Sydney', 'brother in Bay', or rather vaguely, 'sister in New South Wales'. 42 per cent of the males over 14 (i.e. not including dependant children) had relatives in the colony.

61 per cent of the males over 14 could read and write; a further 17 per cent could read only, compared with 52 per cent and 28 per cent for the females. The vast majority of the immigrants claimed to belong to the Church of England, however there were 24 Wesleyans, 8 Roman Catholics (six of them couples from Cornwall but of Irish origin), four Methodists, four Baptists and four Independents, and one Calvinist. They were all of 'good health' except one three year old who was described as 'delicate' and a baby with 'inflamation of lungs'.

The Parsee *in Brisbane, c1856; built in 1851 at St John, New Brunswick, she was owned by Carter and Co, in 1854 her master was J. Akitt. She made a number of voyages to Australia in the 1850s. (By courtesy of Mrs C.Randle).*

125

The average family size in the nineteenth century tended to be considerably larger than that of today, nevertheless it is perhaps surprising to note so many parents willing to undertake such an arduous and uncertain journey with a bevy of toddlers in tow; for example Charles and Grace Randle from East Coker (Somerset), on the *Parsee*, had with them Lot (18), Giles (16), Selina (14), Grace (8), Mary (6) and Emily (1), and a son was born on the voyage.

With such a spirit of adventure, and great bravery, these people from the remotest corners of rural England uprooted themselves and set off full of hope to a land which was, to all intents and purposes, almost unknown to them. Their only preparation and warning were the odd letters home from relatives who had previously taken the plunge, and the cajoling of the agents and their pamphlets – unless, perhaps, they had been lucky enough to experience the *Panorama of Australia*, advertised at the Assembly Rooms, Salisbury and including a staggering 6,500 feet of transparent scenery, on 19 and 20 February, 1831.[47] Otherwise they travelled with little more than courageous expectation in their pockets and in their hearts:

Off we go to Adelaide, as fast as we are able.
Beef and mutton we expect to see upon the table.[48]

7 THE VOYAGE

Ye gentlemen of England, who live at home at ease,
O little do ye know of the troubles of the seas.[1]

The First Fleet spent more than eight months on the voyage from Portsmouth to Botany Bay, stopping off for long spells in Rio de Janeiro and Capetown, almost as if it was reluctant to complete the journey; even the later convict transports took four or five months – between 1788 and 1820 not one completed the passage in less than 112 days, and many of them exceeded 200 days, nearly seven months.[2] Those early vessels were fat and dumpy, 'their hulls were full and round. They could sit almost bolt upright on the mud of a tidal harbour';[3] their bows were blunt, they had a square stern and tended to ride like a cork. From the mid 1840s much sleeker and more elegant 'clippers' competed with one another for the fastest times – they followed the Great Circle route recommended by John Towson in 1847, it was shorter, but required far greater skill of the masters; it demanded frequent changes of direction, and sailing farther south ran the risk of icebergs.[4] In 1852 the *Try* of Bristol, with a party of emigrants from North Devon on board, made the trip in just 92 days; but that was nothing compared to the feat of Captain Godfrey who, in 1850, in the *Constance*, had broken all previous records by reaching Adelaide in 77 days, following the Great Circle route. The rush to the gold fields in the early 1850s encouraged even greater competition with fortune hunters desperate to get there quickly – one Captain Forbes, in the *Marco Polo*, made it to Port Phillip in the incredible time of 68 days, and then returned to England in only 76 days – some vessels were taking as long on a one-way trip as his return journey.

One man with West Country connections whose studies greatly influenced the success of the faster voyages was William Scoresby; in 1832 he was appointed to the Bedford Chapel in Exeter and after a period in Bradford (Yorkshire), he retired to Torquay in 1850, where he lived at Sparkwell Villa (renamed Grosmont) and assisted the incumbent of Upton Church[5]. Throughout his life he continued to work as an active scientist, making a significant contribution to the study of physics and particularly magnetism. New iron-hulled ships were introduced in the 1850s to replace traditional wooden vessels clad in lead, zinc or copper – the cladding was required to protect the timber from the teredo worm, but it was extremely expensive. Iron ships had a number of advantages; most particularly the increase in internal volume, they were also much safer from fire; but they suffered one major and rather alarming handicap: the iron hulls caused a deflection of the magnetic compass. Scoresby reckoned to work out a way of allowing for this discrepancy, and to prove his hypothesis he set out to Australia in 1856, having positioned a second compass in the crow's nest, as far away from the hull as possible. The successful proof of his method allowed iron vessels to follow the Great Circle route without fear of veering madly off course.[6]

Such matters, though, were acedemic to the mass of emigrants from the West Country who either had their passages arranged for them – by their sponsor, be it government agent, parish or individual – or responded to one of the flurry of advertisments that appeared in almost every issue of the local papers. The *Plymouth Devonport and Stonehouse Herald* of Saturday 10 February 1849, for example, carried the following announcement:

Cheap and very superior cabin passage to Port Phillip, Australia Felix.
For Port Phillip direct, under charter to the Government to sail from Plymouth on the 26th instant.
The fine first-class fast-sailing British Built Ship
Hope, A.1.
513 Tons Register. John Gill Commander.
The Poop accomodations in this ship are very lofty, and the cabins unusually large. She carries an experienced surgeon, and is a desirable ship for passengers. For freights or passage apply to Messrs. Lachlan, Macleod, 62 Cornhill, London; Messrs. Pope, Bros., the owners, Plymouth or to
Mr J.B.Wilcocks
The Agent for Emigration
Barbican, Plymouth.
From whom the fullest information relative to the Colonies, Emigration etc. may be obtained gratuitously and by whom passages may be arranged to all parts of the world in thoroughly efficient vessels.

In the same edition of the paper, Mr S.Charles Johnson, emigration, commission and shipping agent, was advertising for passengers to join his ships sailing to Adelaide on 20 and 25 February, for 20 guineas or £42 respectively and in a separate advert Her Majesty's Colonial Land and Emigration Commissioners, here represented by J.B.Wilcocks again, notified 'chief cabin passengers' that the following vessels would be sailing on the dates stated 'guaranteed':[7]

Ship	Tons	Commanders	Date leaving Plymouth	Destination
John Bright	591	Alex McClean	17 Feb	Sydney
Floretia	453	S.S.Tindal	24 Feb	Adelaide
Diana	574	Ellis Fletcher	27 Feb	Sydney
Caroline Agnes	570	A.F.Morris	4 Mar	Port Phillip
Hope	513	John Gill	28 Feb	Port Phillip
Lady Peel	541	R.L.Frazer	3 Mar	Sydney
Elizabeth	569	Jas.Alexander	10 Mar	Port Phillip
Scotia	657	Thos.Stricland	20 Mar	Sydney

An editorial continued by recommending Plymouth as the most convenient port for departure, saving 'the danger, discomfort and annoyance of the Channel passage' and gaining ten days 'for business purposes in England and emigrants of whatever grade generally find they have enough to do at the last moment'.

There certainly was a lot to be done. For cabin passengers a certain amount of negotiation with the Captain was necessary to ensure that they would be adaquately cared for at sea: Francis Gerard Tabart, a one-time clothier of Uley (Gloucestershire) was due to sail with his family in the *Mary* to Van Dieman's Land in 1830 – an agreement of 13 April, with the Captain, William Beachcroft, states that for the sum of £235 he (the Captain) would provide two stern starboard cabins for Mr Tabart, his wife, sister and five children (aged 11, 7, 4, 2 years and 9 months) and would supply them with a sufficient quantity of poultry, fresh and preserved meats, wine, spirits and porter, and other necessary provisions during their passage. He would also receive on board any goods that Mr Tabart did not stow in his cabins at the rate of 50 shillings per ton of 40 cubic feet, and would

agree to convey a Cow to Hobart Town (if Mr Tabart should determine on taking one) and to supply the same with a sufficient quantity of water and necessary accomodation free from any charge for freight etc. for the same, on the milk which she may yield on the passage being appropriated to the use of the passengers, Mr Tabart furnishing the necessary fodder only.[8]

For all passengers there was no shortage of advice on what to pack: the *Dictionary of Medical and Surgical Knowledge and Complete Practical Guide in Health and Disease for families Emigrants and Colonists*, 1850, stated:[9]

> What is chiefly required is a couple of suits of common strong slops, with a sufficiency of linen, worsted and cotton stockings and a few handkerchiefs. Formerly when no washing was permitted during the voyage, the outfit for body linen for both men and women was heavy and expensive; now, however, that two days in the week are allowed for washing much less clothing is required. Both adults and children should wear on board light but not thin-soled shoes, made with buckles or elastic sides, strings being avoided as apt to lead to accidents. In wet, cold weather or whenever the decks are damp, thin cork soles should be worn in the shoes with worsted stockings long enough to cover the knees; at the same time the trousers, waistcoat and the sleeves of the coat should be lined with flannel or pieces of an old blanket. For females, a flannel bandage should be passed around the knees which, with the drawers, the cork soles, and an extra petticoat, will be apparel sufficient.

Other necessities for the voyage were:

> a knife, fork, tea and table spoon, pewter plate, hook pot, pint mug for tea, meat dish, water can, washing basin, scrubbing brush, two cabbage nets, half a gallon of sand, flour bag, Bath brick, two sheets of sand paper, two canvas aprons, hammer and bag of nails, gimlet, long leather straps and buckles to secure the bed on deck when twice a week it is aired, 3 lbs of marine soap.[10]

But the best advice to the emigrant was that he should 'possess a sound constitution, a good stock of animal spirits, a cheerful disposition, to enable him to make light of difficulties, with energy to surmount all the vexations and troubles that may befall'.[11]

Assisted emigrants, once they had arrived in Plymouth, were cared for in the Emigrants' Home free of charge until their vessel was ready to

A Victorian artist's romantic interpretation of the 'leave-taking'; a young man saying goodbye to his family as he is about to depart for a new life in a new world.

sail; others found lodgings in one of the rash of hotels and boarding houses that sprang up to cater for the busy trade.

At last, on the appointed day if the weather was fair, the emigrants were rowed out to their vessel at anchor; and for the first time saw the space that was to be their home for the next five, six or even seven months. The second deck or 'tween deck was that appointed for the steerage passengers:

> the height of the between decks varies from six to seven feet according to the size and build of the vessel. It extends the whole inside breadth of the ship and the berths are fitted along the sides. Each berth contains from two to six beds, one placed above another, that is two people sleeping lengthways with the ship and one, two or four across according to the capacity of the ship. Along the length of the ship a table is placed about two feet and a

half broad, and securely fastened to the deck in case of heavy weather. Along the sides of passenger ships there are spaces cut out at about every seven feet, and fitted with strong glass panes, which can be pushed outwards for the purpose of ventilation. These panes of glass are about six inches in diameter, and the berths are frequently so fitted that one serves as a light for two cabins. Of course these small windows are chiefly useful in heavy rains when it is impossible to open the hatches.[12]

Generally conditions on the emigrant vessels travelling to Australia were far better than those on the much shorter run to North America; emigration to Australia was largely controlled by the British Government whereas private venturers organised the American traffic – with no approved standards. 'Once governments began to select migrants for Australia and to subsidize their fares, they tended to become responsible for their well being during the voyage'.[13] From the 1820s the British

A female emigrants' home, where single women could await the departure of their ship; Illustrated London News, *12 March 1853.*

The Citadel, Plymouth, 1857, J.W.Carmichael (1800-1868); (By courtesy of the City Museum and Art Gallery, Plymouth). The emigrant depot is shown left of centre on the quayside and the larger vessels are possibly emigrant ships.

parliament began to pass Passenger Acts which regulated the conditions in British-owned ships, and whilst on the short trip to America these new laws were laxly enforced, on the voyage to Australia they were applied with vigour.

The area of the ship given over to steerage passengers was divided, for the sake of morality, into three compartments (at least from the 1840s onwards); single women were confined to the stern of the vessel with a heavy bulkhead separating them from the married couples and children

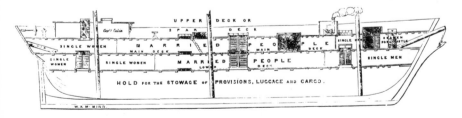

Section through a typical emigrant vessel, showing the division of space and the careful separation of single men from single women.

in the middle; another bulkhead left space for single men towards the prow. Within each section the emigrants formed themselves into messes of ten or so people, to simplify the distribution of rations; before each meal the head of the mess went to the galley to collect the allowance of food for his group and brought it back to be shared out amongst them – for many the food provided on the voyage was far better than anything they had experienced at home:

The daily adult ration included:

8oz   Biscuits
6oz   Pork on 3/7 days, 6oz Preserved meat on other days.
6oz   Flour
3oz   Oatmeal
2oz   Raisins on 4/7 days only.
1½oz Suet on 4/7 days only.
½pint Peas on 3/7 days.
4oz   Rice on 2/7 days.
4oz   Preserved potatoes on 2/7 days.
½oz   Tea on 4/7 days.
½oz   Cocoa nibs on 3/7 days.
4oz   Sugar on 3/7 days.
2oz   Treacle on 4/7 days.
2oz   Butter on 2/7 days.
3 quarts of water 1oz Lime juice with ½oz Sugar
     was served daily to combat scurvy.
In addition there was a weekly allowance of 1 gill of mixed pickles, ½oz. mustard, 2oz salt and ½oz pepper.[14]

Emigrants were advised that a few luxuries might help to relieve the boredom and were recommended to take, if they could afford them, a ham, some good tea, extra pickles, wine, brandy, jam and preserved vegetables.[15]

Various accounts survive of the voyages of West Country emigrants; some full of colourful detail, others mundane descriptions of the weather and dull routine. One of the most vivid was written by John Skinner Prout, nephew of the artist Samuel Prout, who emigrated in about 1840 on the *Royal Sovereign;* his journal was published in London in 1844.[16] John Prout was born in Plymouth in 1806; he lived in Bristol between about 1830 – 1840, working as an artist.[17] The preface describes him as a 'man of education ...who embarked with his wife and seven young children as steerage passengers in the *Royal Sovereign*... for Sydney'; it adds that they did have 'the accomodation of a separate cabin' and that their voyage 'was extended to the unusual length of 136 days'...'in consequence of calms':

> About eight o'clock in the evening we left Plymouth; the sun had set peacefully; the new moon, red with the hues of evening, hung just over Mount Edgecombe, night was gathering round us, and all nature was so beautifully still, that it appeared impossible that causes to make man unhappy, could exist in the country we were then quitting, perhaps for ever; but I had only to remember the continued difficulties and harassment of mind we had experienced during the past two years, to enable me most cheerfully to part with those of my family, then assembled on the beach, to see the last of us....The next morning, Sunday, about four o'clock we were awoke by the noise of the sailors on deck, hoisting sail and raising the anchor; and when I come on deck, at eight o'clock, we were outside the Breakwater, and, in fact had commenced our voyage....After breakfast there was a muster of all the children, and the surgeon [Mr Jones] was most actively employed performing the operation of vaccination.....

> *Monday morning:* ....Our deck presents a most motley group, or rather groups. Most of the lot of emigrants, taken in at Plymouth, sick. One poor girl with her bonnet on hind part before; another with her gown brought over her head, and looking the very personification of misery; children, some crying and some playing; men lying in all positions, and in all situations.

> *Friday:* The increase of heat felt most sensibly, so that we experienced the comfort of the awning which had this day been spread: towards evening delightfully cool – all parties on deck; in the lower deck dancing, singing, and practical jokes; on the poop some admiring the evening; some playing chess, others dominoes, all wishing for a breeze....

> *Wednesday, a day of births:* The Doctor has received notice that his peculiar services will most probably be required; and much to his annoyance the steward [who had made use of the hospital for his sleeping apartment and store room] has orders to shift his quarters immediately, in consequence of which, hams, hammock, preserved tripe, and other epicurean dainties, are walked off to the

Between decks on an emigrant vessel. Illustrated London News, *10 May 1851.*

gun-room, and the mother-expectant, with delectable Mary as nurse, occupy the deserted quarters...... Half-past four; noisy as the surrounding multitude have been, and still are, one little shrill cry has just issued from the quarter in question that has drowned all other sounds and we know that Mr Agar is blessed with a son and heir.

Wednesday and Thursday: ....we had lost sight of the porpoises for many days but this afternoon were delighted to see our old friends surrounding the vessel; word was sent aft that they were under our bows. The dolphin striker was manned. Every part where a peep could be obtained was crowded.....another monster came rolling in towards us, and in an instant the white spray from the bow became crimson with the rush of blood, and we knew that this time the spear had done its duty....the poor fish was soon brought to the edge of the water, the blood issuing in a flood from the wound in its side; but although struck in so deadly a manner its strength was still immense and it was with great difficulty that it was brought on deck ...All now were anxious to possess a share of the spoil; so much salt provisions had made the poor porpoise quite an anticipated luxury and the carvers were besieged by a voracious multitude.

Friday: We are now passing St Antonio, one of the Cape Verd Islands, and about twenty-five miles from it.....

Sunday August 30th: During the past week we have had little else than a succession of squalls accompanied by the heaviest rain I ever witnessed. Wet decks, and wet berths, have no tendency to raise the spirits......there has been little opportunity afforded for going on deck; and the heat below has been intolerable...We hope to cross the line about Tuesday or Wednesday....

Sunday September 13th: The long-expected south-easter is come at last; a beautiful breeze; six and seven knots an hour.

Sunday September 27th: The wind has got back to the N.E. blowing half a gale, and the rain coming down in torrents; we are now, however, able to make our course, and though but few sails are hoisted, going at seven and a half; this is the most wretched day we have had since leaving England. All below is dark and uncomfortable, we being obliged to close our ports forward, the hatches are down, and but few of the steerage passengers venture on deck ....she is rolling tremendously, loose spars and other matters are changing places continually, so that it is scarcely safe to walk about.

Monday: We have passed one of the most miserable nights imaginable, the vessel rolling and plunging, and consequently displacing all our as well as our neighbours' valuables; water-casks and boxes, fragments of bottles, dishes, plates, and cups, all rumbling and rattling about in glorious confusion....above us in the cuddy berths....they have had the water in in such quantities, as to make it impossible for them to remain in bed. To these accumulated comforts, add the almost terrific sounds occasioned by the sea striking and breaking over the ship....the children are all kept to their beds, ports closed – cabins wet – no prospect of getting any thing cooked....

Wednesday: A dead calm!

Friday: ....Between decks the catholics are at their evening devotions: this is a strange scene. The lamp, suspended from the beam, throws its dim light on the countenances of the devotees, who kneeling around one of the mess tables, are apparently quite absorbed in the service read by their appointed priest.....before him is placed a small crucifix, and a tea-cup containing water...

Saturday: Half-past five o'clock this evening was the time selected to perform the last offices to poor Kitty's remains, [Kitty was a young steerage passenger who had died the previous day soon after giving birth to a baby girl] and accordingly at that hour, the body, encased in canvass (sic) and covered with flags as a pall, was brought on deck, and placed on a plank which had been so arranged that it should form an inclined plane, from the lower part of the main-mast to the gangway, projecting over the side of the vessel; the bag of sand was attached to the feet; on either side stood the mate and boatswain, with others of the crew, ready at the given time to raise the end of the plank.....

Sunday 18 October: Mr Marsh's birthday;.....This afternoon our little party occupied and pretty well filled the boatswain's cabin, where a bottle of good brandy, pipes, cigars, enabled us, in a proper manner to do the birthday honours.

Monday: A most fearful night; sleep not to be named. The vessel pitched tremendously, so much so that the captain was most unceremoniously thrown from his bed to the opposite side of his cabin, and was severely cut and bruised....Birds in abundance surround us....

Friday: Poor Kitty L's baby, deprived of a mother's care, had been anything but well for some time past; and this evening being supposed much worse, Mr Jones was hastily summoned to christen it. Such a christening! Instead of the happy faces of the parents and friends......none but strangers stood around and sorrowful indeed were the faces that bent over it as the service was being read......

Saturday: This evening the baby died.

Tuesday: No wind, and a tremendous sea; the vessel almost rolling her yards under the water, and displacing every moveable article in the cabins. Water barrels break through their fastenings, and rolling from side to side, pour their liquid treasures on the floor and form a syrup with the emptied contents of dislodged sugar cans; candlesticks, work-boxes, and writing-desks, hats, bonnets, bustles, and petticoats.....

Wednesday 11 November: ....We hoped to see St Paul's about six in the evening, but were far from being displeased at our being summoned three hours earlier. It is near three months since we were blest with a sight of our mother earth, and therefore it will be easily imagined with what a relish we enjoyed our first sight of the island, which was then about twenty miles to the east of us.

Emigrants at dinner; note the sleeping berths on either side, children slept above, parents below; the space allowed was 3 feet by 6 feet. Illustrated London News, *13 April 1844.*

Wednesday: This morning at half-past four received the expected announcement that we were off the land; we had at last arrived at the entrance of the Straits; the land we had then made....was Cape Otway, a part of Australia...

Tuesday: ....At one o'clock we were between Sydney Heads, but unfortunately the night became cloudy, and consequently the moon was of little service to us. We had fired a gun three times as signal for a pilot, and just before we reached the inner light, placed on a group of rocks known by the elegant name of 'Sow and Pigs', a boat was seen approaching us. The pilot came on board, and in a few minutes our Captain was no longer commander. We were now in a narrow passage, high cliffs rising on one side, and apparently thickly-wooded headlands on the other.....In another hour day broke, and the lovely harbour, beautiful islands, and distant town of Sydney, were seen before us. After so long an absence from land, the scene appeared one of enchantment-......Soon the healthy-men came on board; we were declared all right, and free to land as we pleased.

In other accounts there is a greater element of self-entertainment to relieve the boredom; George Rowe, for example, on the *Panama* in 1852, made sketches which he sold, helped to organise musical and theatrical evenings for the passengers and was chosen to act as Master of Ceremonies at the celebrations held to mark the crossing of the equator.[18] John Joseland in his journal of the voyage of the *Salsette* in 1853 described the activities in detail:[19]

Saturday 23 April: ....At 10 o'clock the crew, with their faces blackened, or painted, and dressed in all sorts of colours, headed by one of the stewards, in a red shirt, with a black feather in his cap, part of a newspaper as a book, a stick as a pen in his hand to perform the part of barber's clerk, then the boatswain disguised and attired in a most fantastic style, riding upon the backs of some of the sailors (who stooped down to appear like a mule) in the character of Neptune, went all round the ship before the performance of shaving etc. commenced. This began with the crew, so they had the advantage of clean water. The Barber stands before the tub, upon which the person sits who is acted upon. His clerk sits by the side to put down what he says, which part, however, he generally neglects doing. Then a dialogue takes place. Clerk 'Where do you come from?' He opens his mouth to speak and in goes the barber's lather brush! 'Where were you born?' In goes the brush again. 'Have you got your passport?' 'Have you ever crossed the Line?' If the person does not answer, the Clerk gives him a stripe or two with a wet 'Swob' which is a kind of mop they use to dry up the decks after washing them. It is made of untwisted rope, or rather yarn, in the shape of a horse's tail, only larger. The Clerk then tells him he must 'be shaved' which operation the Barber performs with Tar and Grease generally, but this time lather was used, which he scrapes off with a piece of iron hoop notched on the edge. He then gives him a push and over he goes head over heels into a Sheet of Water a few feet below, holding about a Hogshead, perhaps more. Where there are two waiting to duck him! All the sailors, with two exceptions, had to undergo the operation. Then came the passengers who, one after another, did the same except myself, Mrs Dunne, Mr Walsh and the Doctor. We paid the fine:- a bottle of brandy.

John and Martha Joseland, travelling in some style in a cabin, suffered a particularly stormy voyage in a very leaky vessel:

Sunday 24 April: The wind blowing South East, our course lying almost due East but sailing from necessity South West, causes our sails to be so set that we can lie as close to the wind as possible which, in consequence, throws us over on our Starboard side considerably. Our cabin being on the Larboard is extremely uncomfortable, our bed being sometimes so steep that it is difficult to keep in any way....

Wednesday 27 April:...we are sailing at the rate of 7 knots all day with little inconvenience except that at meals we are obliged to eat with our plates in our hands and drink our coffee and tea after. Even then we seldom sit down without having a few mishaps, in the shape of upsetting our cups and plates into the laps of those opposite us.......I have so packed my boxes that unless the ship goes right over they will not stir.

......We are now rounding the Cape.

Tuesday 24 May: ...About 12 o'clock a very heavy cross sea commenced rolling which caused the ship to lurch fearfully. We were awoke by the noise of boxes casks etc., getting adrift and rolling from one side to another as if determined to break down our partitions. Then again the breaking of bottles in the cabin, the crockery in the pantry, the upsetting of water pails, basins etc.. I got up and found the greatest confusion. Some of the passengers were in a dreadful state, their luggage and all pell mell over the place. Our boxes were so locked and bottles etc., so packed that they did not stir so Martha lay, or rather sat, up in bed and regaled herself at the expense of the poor unfortunates by laughing at their calamities.

Tuesday 7 June: at day break the gale increased so much that the Capt gave orders for the ship to be hove to. All canvas was immediately stowed except the Main Top Sail. In this condition we lay all day and night during which time it blew fearfully especially at night when it was a perfect hurricane. The motion was very great and in addition the ship made a great deal of water so much so that the pumps were scarcely left the whole time passengers and all taking their places at them....Our cabins were completely flooded Martha was obliged to lie or sit upon the bed the whole of the day time.

Monday 20 June: ....the ship was making so much water that we were obliged to be at the pumps 20 minutes out of every half hour all that day and night, the remainder of our time on deck by day being spent in teasing oakum that is pulling rope yarns into shreds for stopping the leaks we could discover.

Saturday 25 June: We begin to find a great difference in the atmosphere and climate now. As we approach the coast it is more genial and pleasant than it has been at any other part of the voyage....

Sunday 26 June: ...in the evening just before dark another leak was discovered in the Bow and one also in the Stern, both very awkward places, below water and impossible to get at outside. It would be dangerous too inside for the carpenter would have to cut way in both instances a good deal of the most important ties in that part of the ship in order to get at it....I hope we shall soon be able to get clear of her [the ship] altogether for I am sick and tired of living in a place not fit for pigs and being kept on diet which is far inferior to what would be had in a convict ship.

Tuesday 5 July:...Soon after ten from the Man aloft we heard 'Land' Oh how all eyes were strained in the direction to which he pointed and how pleasant did the sight appear as the Land opened up gradually....I have looked up at many places from the sea but certainly never saw so lovely a sight as was presented at this time.

The Captain put in to Williamstown to try and replenish the stocks of fresh meat, but the passengers, compelled to stay on board, though only half a mile from shore, felt increasingly frustrated. John Joseland managed to hail a passing mail steamer and leapt at the opportunity to explore ashore; he was landed at Sandridge. In order to return to the *Salsette* he had to bargain ferociously with the boatmen – the first demanded three pounds for the half-hour trip; in the end he reluctantly paid a sovereign.

They finally managed to leave the ship when the Captain arranged for a steamer to come out and carry the passengers and their luggage to Melbourne; Joseland's parting comment summed up his feelings about the journey: 'We soon got on board and left the ship which had been our home for nearly five long months. I believe firmly that no body of passengers ever left a ship with a fewer regrets and a greater feeling of disgust than we did'.

If life on an emigrant vessel could be hard for the passengers, it was invariably the more so for the crew. Unfortunately few crewmen had either the aptitude or opportunity to keep full records of their experiences, but one interesting account survives in a very down-to-earth diary of a voyage made in 1853 on the *Elizabeth* sailing from Plymouth to Port Phillip between January and May; the stained pages are bound in leather, rubbed smooth and polished over time. The National Maritime Museum catalogue refers to it as 'kept by emigrants', but the text suggests that it was probably written by a steward – or at least someone who had closer contact with the crew:[20]

26 Jan: ..a heavy swell from the north west which makes our ship roll heavily and the passengers are all very sick.

29 Jan: This evening the mate gave us a bottle of grog it being his birthday. 8am Served the passengers water out from which they grumbled at the shortness of the allowance. One of the passengers whose name is Mr Nichole's and Mr Walker have propose(d) to print a paper called the *Tropical Times.*

30 Jan: Prayers on board the ship. the Doctor officiated and a poor hand he made of it.

1 Feb: Received the first lime juice and vinegar, rice again today being twice following. Complained to the mate about the pork which altho good it run very short after careful enquiry he promised to better it for the future.

2 Feb: This afternoon the crew mustered aft for tobacco when the Capn. told us he would serve out no more without ready money which he very well know was impossible thus depriving us of the only comfort we have on board and every prospect of a long passage.

4 Feb: At dinner time one of the crew wrote a letter to the passengers of the second cabin for a subscription to get some tobacco which they very well succeeded and is going to give us a ½lb every fortnight while it last.

The Marco Polo *built by Smith and Co., St John, New Brunswick. In 1852, under Capt. James Nicol Forbes, she halved the passage time to Australia, carrying 930 emigrants from Liverpool to Melbourne in 68 days, following the composite great circle route.* Illustrated London News, *19 February 1853.*

5 Feb: ..the watch served the passengers flour out of which they grumbled about the shortage of the allowance which the purser measured instead of weighing it. This day the paper came out called the *Tropical Times* and a very good thing it is.

6 Feb: At 1pm the mate allowed us to wash our cloths this afternoon.

9 Feb: All hands variously employed great murmuring with the passengers about the Doctor they think he is not fit for 'is station – which it is the crews opinion too.

14 Feb: the mate gave orders to get all ready for Neptune to come on board which he did about 2pm when we had fine sport it being nearly calm. The cook is very ill and we do not expect that he will live.

15 Feb: 3 of the men laid up with cramp in their stomachs which we have all had a touch of. Very hot.

16 Feb: One of the passengers Mrs Pascoe died after a long illness of sea sickness and through the neglect of the doctor.....The passengers grumbled at the mate about the shortness of the water and the mate 'as promised them that they should have their full allowance of water.

18 Feb: Passengers making good use of the rain water while they can in washing out their dirty clothes.

20 Feb: We have one of our men in a fever but I hope he will soon get over it. This evening being Saturday the mate sent forward a bottle of grog.

21 Feb: the second mate had the boys on drill this afternoon for not serving out water for the passengers in the forenoon. There is a great quantity of bread bad which we got some on deck and dry'd it and picked out the bad.

26 Feb: The mate jumped overboard for a larck after which the passengers did the same and then the mate put the boys overboard. Trinidad Island.

3 Mar: We are very badly off for we have got no tobacco for we had none since we left England from the Capt. and have been on the generosity of the passengers, and now they cannot get any not for another week.

6 Mar: Part of the crew had a bathe over the side some with life preservers and life buoys.

10 Mar: There was a raffel amongst the passengers for some cheeses and it went of very fast at 6oz......the cheese I believe belongs to the mate.

13 Mar: This afternoon we sent after our lime juice and there was none up but the Capt. being there he said we should have some tomorrow.

20 Mar: it is now going on for 3 weeks since we got any [lime juice].

28 Mar: The passengers had some amusements which they have every Monday they acted a farce got up by one of the passengers named Mr Richards called the Misers which went off very well after which they sang a few songs.

20 Apr: Great talk with the passengers about seeing land on Saturday.

Joseland's journal[21] recorded the punishment of a crew member:

Saturday 26 March: ....This evening one of the crew disobeyed orders. He was instantly seized by the Mate, while the Captain tied his hands behind him 'gagged him' which is, to put a piece of wood about a foot long and 1½" diameter in his mouth, then this is tied at the back of his neck so that he could not move his head round. He was then made to walk to the fore part of the vessel and mount a platform, where they generally have to sit without food for some 8 or 10 hours – but owing to the intervention of one of the Owners, he was released after 2 hours. My English blood boiled when I saw the poor fellow 'gagged' but I am told it is a thing of no rare occurence at sea.

One of the least conventional voyages, inspired by the lure of gold, was that undertaken by seven young fishermen from Newlyn (Cornwall) in 1854.[22] Presumably unable to afford even a steerage passage, these young men, led by Richard Nicholls, sailed their fishing lugger *Mystery* to Australia. The boat was only 33 feet long, and 11 feet 6 inches in the beam, and weighed just ten tons. Anyway they set off on 18 November; it was reported that the inhabitants of Cape Town were so impressed by the pluck of the adventurers and the seaworthiness of the lugger, that the authorities entrusted Her Majesty's Mail to their care. After riding out several gales they reached Hobson's Bay, Melbourne, on 14 March 1855, a voyage of 116 days. The *Mystery* was sold soon after their arrival. Another party of Cornishmen attempted the same journey in a similarly tiny vessel, the *Snowdrop*, but after putting-in at the Galapagos Islands for water, they were never seen again.[23]

Model of the Mystery, *a fishing lugger of only 10 tons, which was sailed to Australia in 1854 by seven young Newlyn fishermen. (Courtesy of the Royal Institution of Cornwall).*

147

Despite the relatively favourable statistics, compared with the shorter Atlantic crossing, there are numerable examples of tragedy on emigration voyages; icebergs and heavy seas in the high latitudes down south claimed their toll, as did the treacherous Channel coastline of Dorset, Devon and Cornwall. On the foul night of the 25 November 1871 the storm-bucket was up on the signal mast at Portland Bill indicating gale force winds from the south-west; lashing waves pounded the cliffs and roared on the steep, eight-mile-long, shingle bank of Chesil Beach. The *Royal Adelaide*, a 2,000 ton emigrant clipper, only a few hours out from Portsmouth, was quite helpless and was driven onto the shingle, where the waves continued to break over her decks and pound her sides. As the vessel broke up, locals rushed to help with life-lines and ropes; 60 people were saved, seven drowned. The most poignant relics of the disaster are three tiny pairs of infants' shoes, a candle and a fork – now displayed in the Portland Museum.

The *Royal Adelaide* happened to be carrying a cargo of spirits, in addition to the emigrants, and the rescuers were not slow to avail themselves of the barrels that washed ashore; it is said that two died, not from drowning in the swell nor being swept out to sea, but from drunkenness and exposure.[24] Another legend associated with this wreck tells of 'the naked body of a most beautiful woman' washed up on the beach the following day; looters were preparing to sever her fingers to remove her rings when a stranger arrived in a coach and took the body away. Her sudden revival and their later marriage only improves the story.[25]

Another victim of Chesil Beach was the *Lanoma*, wrecked near Fleet on 8 March 1888 in thick fog; she had endured a difficult voyage all the way from Van Dieman's Land, carrying a cargo of wool. Her Captain and crew perished and for days afterwards the beach was littered with sodden fleeces.[26]

Charles Medyett Goodridge, from Paignton (Devon), found his way to Van Dieman's Land literally by accident:[27] he sailed as an ordinary mariner on the *Princess of Wales* to the South Seas in search of skins, whale oil, fins and ambergris. The vessel was a cutter of 75 tons, with Captain William Veale as Commander; they left London on 1 May 1820. After a hair-raising adventure pursuing seals around the Prince Edward Islands, the *Princess of Wales* was wrecked one stormy night when she struck some rocks 'with tremendous force'. The crew took to the lifeboat....

The frontispiece to Charles Goodridge's account of his shipwreck, showing the author in his seal skin costume, published 1838.

The night was dark, rainy and boisterous and the sea dashed over the rocks by which they were surrounded. They found the shore to be much nearer than they expected, but could not land as it was bounded by perpendicular rock. After rowing about for nearly four hours they came into a sort of cove where they got in shore safely, but the boat was swamped. How they escaped the rocks in the darkness and heavy seas was afterwards a matter of astonishment to them. They hauled up the boat, turned it over and got under it....

The men sheltered under the dingy for three weeks, living chiefly on birds and the tongues and hearts of sea elephants which were, apparently, unable to escape the blows and stabs of their crude cudgels.

At the expiration of that time they collected all the timber they could find, for the island did not produce a shrub. With a part of these materials, and some stones, at the end of a few weeks they completed a house and shed.....They hunted seals and sea elephants. The latter animals were their chief subsistence and to use the expression of one of the salors, it was 'meat, drink, fire and lodging to them'....

Incredibly they survived for 22 months until an American schooner, the *Philo*, also sealing, chanced upon them and rescued them. Eventually Goodridge arrived in Hobart Town, where he was taken in by Dr E.Brombley to recover from scurvy. He did not return to his homeland until July 1831 – moored in Torbay, he wrote:

I was in sight of my native village – my heart beat high against my breast, as if it were eager to meet the scenes from which it had been so long separated, ere the means were ready to convey its owner to the fondly cherished spot which had sheltered his early days. The venerable tower of Paignton forming as it does one of the most conspicuous objects in the bay, was full in view....'

Of course during the nineteenth century major advances were made in the design and nature of sea transport; the conversion to steam power, for example, reduced the journey time to Australia to weeks rather than months, and for the first time passenger vessels were no longer subject to the vagueries of the wind and weather. The invention of the screw propeller as a substitute for the wooden paddle revolutionised the potential of steam on the Australian run[28] The steamer *Great Britain,* one of the largest ships in the world at that time and the first to be both built of iron and fitted with a screw propeller, was launched in Bristol on 19 July 1843; she had been built following the success of Brunel's *Great Western,* to compete on the trans Atlantic trip.[29] Prince Albert was guest of honour at the launch and enjoyed a sumptuous cold banquet in a royal pavillion, erected for the day, by the entrance to the dock.

In 1852, under Captain John Gray, she began a career of nearly a quarter of a century carrying emigrants to Australia. On her first trip, from Liverpool, she carried 630 passengers and a crew of 137. First class passengers paid 70 guineas for their passage, but steerage accomodation

Launch of the Great Britain *in Bristol;* Illustrated London News, *27 July 1843.*

was also available at only 14-16 guineas. She reached Melbourne in just over 80 days, and huge crowds flocked to gawp at her from the quay, some paying 2s.6d. for the privilege of walking her decks.[30] One passenger who recorded his enjoyment of the pleasures to be had on board was the Very Rev. Thomas Braim, returning home after serving as Archdeacon to the diocese of Melbourne:[31]

> I came home in the noble steamer the *Great Britain,* and there were nearly 900 of us on board. Everything was managed most admirably: the living like that in a large hotel, a German band played upon the deck, and music and singing and dancing and private theatricals seemed to enable the passengers to pass the time right merrily.

In total *Great Britain* made 32 round trips to Australia, and it is estimated that she carried out more than 10,000 emigrants. In February 1876, back in Liverpool, she was condemned by Lloyd's surveyors and was no longer allowed to carry passengers; but her working life continued until May 1886 when she ended up as a storehouse for wool in Stanley Harbour, Falkland Islands.[32]

Now back in Bristol once again, the *Great Britain* is being restored to her original state, in the dock where she was first built.

> Six masts – like princely sons to bear!
> *Great Britain* for my name
> My smoke trail black on the sun bright air
> My screw as swift and my sails as fair
> As the trumpet voice of Fame![33]

8 FREE SETTLERS

The rural poor, the bulk of the emigrants from the West Country, carried with them a host of skills and experiences which they attempted to apply in their new environment with varying degrees of success; many of the free settlers who had upped and left at their own volition were innovative characters looking for a chance to make good – if their home country was unable to offer them a decent living, then they would strive to carve one out for themselves in Australia. It was certainly not easy; although stories of those who made it abound, there were countless others who continued their existence in this new world just to scrape along between subsistence and starvation. But the new country offered incredible opportunities, and for those who fell lucky, or worked that extra bit hard, comfort and prosperity could be just around the corner.

John Macarthur, baptised at Stoke Damerel, near Plymouth in 1767, was a young lieutenant in the Second Fleet; he arrived in Port Jackson in 1790 with his wife Elizabeth, née Veale, the daughter of a Devon farmer, and their first child, Edward; a daughter born on the voyage did not survive[1] Macarthur was extraordinarily sharp and quickly and unpopularly established himself by profitting from the New South Wales Corps' monopoly on the rum trade; later as Regimental paymaster and Inspector of Public Works he controlled the supply of convict labour and made certain that a lot of it came his way. Through the generous encouragement of Acting-governor Francis Grose, he acquired grants of land at Parramatta, 'some of the best ground that has been discovered' and by 1800 was acknowledged as the wealthiest man in the colony. After a duel with his commanding officer, Macarthur was returned to England in 1801 to face trial, but for lack of information the matter was dropped and he used his time instead to discuss the possibility of exporting wool to English clothiers. Much credit should go to Elizabeth, who in his absence defended the family farm against a convict uprising[2], and shrewdly managed the improvement of their flock. She was an enthusiast for the colony, despite her isolation and wrote home that their house at Parramatta, Elizabeth Farm, was:[3]

a very excellent brick building...We enjoy here one of the finest climates in the world. The necessaries of life are abundant, and a fruitful soil affords us many luxuries. Nothing induces me to wish for a change but the difficulty of educating our children....Our gardens with fruit and vegetables are extensive; and produce abundantly. It is now Spring, and the eye is delighted with a most beautiful variegated landscape; almonds, apricots, pear and apple trees are in full bloom; the native shrubs are also in flower, and the whole country gives a grateful perfume.

Many early settlers benefitted from the availabilty of 'free' labour in the form of assigned convicts, and were able to set themselves up remarkably quickly. Francis Tabart, the Uley clothier, and his family arrived in Van Dieman's Land in 1830; having travelled in relative comfort as cabin passengers, they were presumably considerably better off than the average emigrant. Their first home was a log cabin at Fonthill,[4] in the Oatlands district, but within ten years their estate included an area of 4,000 acres, 300 of which were cultivated, the remainder being forest and rough pasture.[5] The Tabarts had a flock of 10,000 sheep – under the care of ten shepherds, each responsible for a thousand; there were a dozen or more men employed on the rest of the farm, besides a hostler, a butler, a cook, a gardener and two kitchen maids; and work had commenced on building a large stone house. William Gates, a ticket-of-leave convict restricted to the Oatlands district, was recommended to Tabart and worked for him for a year for £8 – in his *Recollections* he wrote:[6]

Tabart was a man of about fifty-five years – had a family, consisting of a wife, two sons, and four daughters. The girls were ordinarily handsome, and to men in our situation quite affable. There, particularly for a woman, to speak with a prisoner, is considered a disgrace....From Tabart and his whole family I received quite fair treatment .....Apparently I was thought much of by him, and was accordingly advanced to the overseership when I had been with him three months. This change relieved me of much toil and promoted me to a residence in the house, where I had far better fare than I had yet experienced.

Tabart was clearly a good judge of character for he sent Gates to Hobart Town to sell his wool; at one point Gates had $5,000 in his pocket and was 'sorely tempted' to make a run for it – but he did not, and returned with the money to his master.

Whilst such older and more experienced emigrants were able to organise themselves efficiently, many young ones struggled to decide just what to do; the possibilities seemed boundless, and they were spoilt for choice. A series of letters written home by one young emigrant from Baltonsborough (Somerset), from a prosperous farming family, inspired one suspects by the achievements of James Austin and John Earle, graphically illustrates the problems of indecision[7]; Thomas Norris had arrived in Victoria with three friends in 1862:[8]

> It is our present intention (that is myself, H.Beak, Lea Maidment, and A.Hill) to make a start for Queensland soon after next shearing, which will be the latter part of November or the beginning of December. You mentioned in your letter it would be quite unsafe to go there on account of the blacks, but do not believe it.... for my part I think it will be a better speculation to go there than to remain in Victoria. 20.4.1862

Francis Tabart's log cabin at Fonthill, Oatlands District, Van Dieman's Land, built c1831, photographed in 1970. (By courtesy of Jane Evans).

155

Portrait of Francis Gerard Tabart as a purser in the Royal Navy, c.1810; in recognition of his service he was recommended for a grant of land in Van Dieman's Land when he emigrated in 1830.
(By courtesy of Anthony Tabart and Jane Evans).

They planned to join a Mr H. who was going to Brisbane to buy land, and would then go up to the Darling Downs to acquire sheep. In order to participate in the enterprise Thomas had to write to his father requesting £500 being his share of the project, and subsequent letters attempted to satisfy his father's enquiries about the safety of the money and the risk of the enterprise.

Meanwhile they moved up to Rockhampton to help a Mr Lowe; writing from Ascot Mills he says:

We find the most of the new country badly watered, particularly that which is not already taken up, and the expense of sinking wells, making dams, and other things very great, so we think the best thing for us to do is to go 'Water hole squatting' for two or three years, of course it will not be quite so comfortable, the expenses will not be so great, and the profits will be greater, that is the main thing. If we have any luck at all, this is the most paying game I know. 23.6.1863.

Thomas also recorded his disappointment that the cash had not yet arrived, despite his lengthy reassurances. Still at Ascot Mills in September 1863 he again wrote to his father to tell of another change of plan:

...our views are frustrated respecting our future undertakings...[two months ago] I intended going back on Mr Lowe's station for a time, but a few days before my departure I heard of a party in Ballarat about to proceed to the Gulf of Carpentaria [overland] and having a wish to go there myself, I at once started back to town, had a conversation with the party respecting the undertaking and I am pleased to say it was then agreed upon we should travle together as one party and all expenses put in to one account.....
20.9.1863.

He explained how they were preparing for the trip, and planning to take 4,000 sheep with them to form a sheep station 'near a seaport' – goodness knows quite where he had in mind – 'I have considered the thing over .... and cannot think of anything more suitable....' He reckoned to be out of contact for at least 12 months, but was optimistic that he would then be back to get some more sheep. In November the £500 arrived safely and he wrote to thank his father saying that the money was not required for his present expedition, so it would be left in safe hands 'at interest' in Melbourne.

By the time the venturers reached Swan Hill in December, things had begun to go wrong – a disease, 'the Pluro', had broken out amongst the bullocks hauling the waggon train, seven had died already and others were looking thin and poor; there were also problems in getting the right sheep at a fair price; but they were able to take some comfort from the fact that they had not plumped immediately for the Darling Downs – there the weather had been so bad, with torrential rains, that half a million sheep had drowned or been destroyed.

157

AUSTRALIA BOUND

In November 1864 they were at the Darling River with 3,700 ewes – lambing; the only problem was that they did not have a water frontage and so were forced to cart water to their flock. 'Many lambs', he wrote, 'were lost to the native wild dogs'. They also heard that the Queensland Government had passed an act forbidding the transfer of sheep across its borders, so:

> ...we, as well as many other parties, are prevented [from getting to the Gulf], if we could get country in New South Wales at a reasonable price we should purchase, but there are so many people on the same tack as ourselves....I hope that we shall get something soon for not having country and no particular object in view, is far from cheering I can assure you...   November 1864

Poor Thomas' difficulties and uncertainties continued; he kept his sheep for a further year but was increasingly tempted to sell up. In one letter, to his brother Henry (14.4.1865) he described the wages paid to labourers – 'This is the place for a labouring man to save money if he choses' – shepherds had 20-25 shillings a week, and even the bullock

Hand shearing and baling wool on a Victorian sheep station.

driver got 25s. He added 'as soon as they have what they term a big cheque, off to the first public house and knock it down. I have known men spend £100 in two weeks, come away 'Fly blown' as they call it, that is without sixpence in their pocket'.

The final letter of the series, to his father, and dated 30 June 1865, sums up his feelings: 'Dear Father, it is not my intention of returning home for some time at any rate, I believe there is a chance for us yet, the difficulty is to make a start'.

It was the experienced farmers who really were able to make a go of it; they knew both what they wanted to do, and how to do it – and very quickly they won the confidence of those around them. One West Country farmer, no doubt benefitting from his experience back home, was awarded three covetted silver tankards at the Cross Marsh Agricultural Society shows, Van Dieman's Land, between 1836-9, for the finest woolled rams[9] – John Bisdee from Hutton (Avon); another, from the heart of the West Country apple growing country, is credited with the introduction of fruit trees to the Stanthorpe area of Queensland, now a principal apple growing area in its own right – George Brownjohn.[10] A pioneer dairy farmer in Victoria, T.J.Sumner, who clearly knew what he wanted, imported the first Jersey cow in 1854 to improve his herd – it was selected for him, in the island, by a Mr J.F.Boodle[11] Captain William Langdon, from Montacute (Somerset), with perhaps more enthusiasm for sport than farming, attempted to introduce pheasants, partridges and other game birds, salmon, trout and tench – he also took out a number of trees and shrubs, including willows.[12]

Thomas Austin, another of that famous Baltonsborough family, will be for ever cursed for his imprudent introduction of rabbits to Australia;[13] he cannot be blamed alone, for the Hentys, Edward and Francis, also imported some and a Mrs Kirkland took a pair to her Western District Station, Trawalla. By the 1850s rabbits had become a serious pest in Victoria.

The impact in Australia of one West Country farmer remains outstanding – this was George Hall Peppin, from Old Shute Farm, Dulverton (Somerset). George's father, also George, and other local Peppins had achieved some fame as breeders of prize stock;[14] one of the family, it is said, was a member of King George III's Household Cavalry and used his influence to persuade the King to import Spanish Merinos into England – some of which eventually found their way to Old Shute

Farm. Here, George senior experimented with cross breeding to produce a bigger and heavier-cutting fine-wool sheep, which came to be called the 'English Merino'.[15]

At the age of 50, with such a background, it is hard to imagine why George junior decided to emigrate, together with his wife, Harriet (née Thompson), and two sons, George and Frederick. They left Plymouth on the *Anna Maria* on 15 August 1850, bound for Melbourne.

George Peppin took up the lease of a sheep run called Mimamaluke, on the south side of the Devil's River, Victoria, in 1851; it was a wet and cold country and his sheep were attacked by fluke, foot-rot and other diseases – by all accounts they were not sorry to move out:

> Of sheep I got a famous lot –
> Some died of hunger, some of rot,
> For the devil a drop of rain they got
> In this flourishing land of Australia. Anon.

Old Shute Farm, near Dulverton, Somerset, the birthplace and home of George Hall Peppin. (By courtesy of Mr Ridgeway).

George Hall Peppin and his
wife, c1860.

In 1858 they purchased the South Wanganella Station, 28 miles north of Deniliquin, in the Riverina district, from William Brodribb for £10,000, with a mortgage of £7,000, repayable over four years – some task.

Until the Peppins arrived, the Merino sheep in Australia had not increased in size or wool-carrying capacity since the days of John Macarthur in the early 1800s, when the average weight of wool per sheep was less than six pounds. A Peppin family diary for the year 1859 recorded that the average weight of washed wool off their initial 7,500 sheep was only 3lbs 2½oz;[16] but George, the wily old farmer, struggled on and set about selecting sheep from other stations in the neighbourhood and improving his property. With such heavy debts and poor returns on their sheep, and countless days wasted in searching for lost stock on their unfenced land, things got pretty desperate – perhaps they would have been wiser to stay on at Old Shute after all; the *Melbourne Argus* of 13 July 1861 carried the following advertisment:[17]

Important Notice – Messrs Peppin and Sons, of South Wanganella, Billabong, having decided on returning to England, have instructed us to treat privately for the Sale of the above Station, together with 20,000 sheep. To any person anxious to embark in this description of property we would only state that, considering the well-known character of the run, the quality of the sheep, the extent of the improvements, we know of no place in the market to equal it....

...but there were no offers, so there was nothing for it but to return to the Station and try to revive their fortunes by breeding a type of sheep more suitable to the district.

In August 1862 a correspondent in the *Pastoral Times* wrote[18] of his visit to..

..the property of Peppin and Sons, who have the reputation of owning sheep equal in bulk and quality to any in the district. Judging from the prices their fat sheep have realised on the Melbourne market the statement appears well founded. The homestead wears an air of comfort and from a slight knowledge of the head of the family I should think that he would be content with nothing less than the 'imperium in impero' – Every Englishman's home is his castle – a free translation. The head of the house is certainly the finest sample of the old English gentleman whom I have seen in the Colonies.

'*Emperor*', *the Rambouillet ram, imported to Australia in 1865, and purchased by the Peppins to improve their stock.*

With George Hall Peppin of such good stock, his sheep were improving too – the family had increased their land holdings by acquiring another station at Morago, and later one at Borothat. By continuous careful selection and breeding the Peppins managed to produce a large, strong-wooled sheep, capable of walking long distances to water, and of enduring extreme heat without discomfort – priceless attributes in this tough country. In 1864 Peppin and Sons exhibited six pens of sheep at the first Echuca Agricultural Show and were awarded four first prizes and one second.

There are no written records of precisely what mix of breeds were so successfully intermingled to produce the 'Peppin Merino' – experts have suggested some Rambouillet blood, and certainly one particular Rambouillet ram, 'Emperor', who annually yielded 25 pounds of greasy wool, was Peppin's pride and joy; young George added a touch of American stock, Old Grimes from Vermont, with his purchase of a 'handsome ram' from Mr J.H.Clough for the fabulous sum of 250 guineas in 1866; and for good measure a couple of Negretti rams were used. Whatever the recipe, it produced the right result – by 1870 the Peppins had doubled the size of the old-fashioned Merinos and, still more important, had doubled the weight of wool shorn from their new breed. The greater size and strength of their beasts opened up a whole new territory to sheep farming which previously had been rejected as useless outback.

In April 1872 George Hall Peppin died, on his station at Wanganella; the *Pastoral Times* obituary describes an old man who never quite came to terms with life 'down under':[19]

> Though the family have been many years in Australia, the head of the house of Peppin and Sons, whose death we now chronicle, could hardly be acclimatised – the roots of the old oak had penetrated too deeply and firmly into the soil of Old England, and though the tree was transplanted to Australia it was only for a time that it indicated a desire to accomodate itself to antipodean life. Mr Peppin was full of hospitality – of a genial disposition, and his death will be regretted. Mr Peppin's remains were interred in the burying ground of the English church [at Deniliquin]....

The two sons, George and Frederick, continued to improve the stock, forming the foundation of what became the famous 'Double Stud'; in 1876 George died in Melbourne shortly after returning from a visit to England; two years later Frederick pulled out of Wanganella and moved to Melbourne – he was involved with the Australian Frozen Meat Export Company and numerous other agricultural businesses, but also bred Exmoor ponies and Jersey cattle on his farm at Epping, near Melbourne. He died in 1911.

By the middle of the twentieth century, with something in the region of 115 million sheep in the country, it was reckoned that 80 per cent were of the Peppin blood.[20] In March 1965 the Peppins' contribution to the development of the sheep industry in Australia was publicly acknowledged when a magnificent bronze statue of a ram, mounted on a granite base, was unveiled by Lord Casey, on the roadside at Wanganella, in the presence of four descendants of George Hall Peppin and various local dignitaries.[21]

The vast majority of emigrants never hit the front pages of their local papers either during or after their lifetimes; like their counterparts in England and elsewhere records of their lives can often only be pieced together from a handful of official records – births, marriages and the like – and occasionally, should they have gone astray, from court reports.

Charles Cox was the bastard child of Ann Cox of Long Sutton (Somerset), baptised on 18 July 1830; at the age of 22 he married Mary Tottle, a pipemaker, from Stoke St Gregory. In 1857 Charles and Mary, with their baby daughter Emily, boarded the *Irene* for Moreton Bay – Charles was a labourer, and apparently found work in the Upper Freestone Creek area not far from Warwick. Four more children were baptised, Thomas, Ann, Albert and George, but nothing else is known of Charles' life until 4 May 1866.[22]

On that day Charles Cox appeared before the magistrate in Warwick, no details of the case are known, but he was obviously not greatly enamoured by the verdict and went off to John Flemings Hotel where he spent the next four or five hours. A Magisterial Enquiry, held the following day, heard the evidence of Thomas Fowell describing what happened next:[23]

> about 20 minutes past four on yesterday the 4th May I was in the yard at the back of the Telegraph Office. I heard a horseman coming up the street at a very rapid pace – looked round and saw a man on horseback nearly unseated – he was out of its saddle and had one leg on the top of the saddle. I then heard the Horse stumble but I could not see it at that moment. I ran out of the yard – the Horse was galloping away, but the man that I saw nearly

unseated was lying on the Road near a Stone Gutter. I went over to him and my impression was that his brains and blood were lying around him. I saw the blood, it was not a minute after I had seen the Horse pass that I saw the Body on the ground – I have seen a dead body in the watch house – it is the same person I saw riding past my House...

Following the unfortunate death of her husband, Mary Cox came into her own – she practised as a midwife and by 1868 she had saved enough money to buy some land; at that time the huge holdings claimed by squatters were in the process of being broken up and sold under the Crown Land Alienation Act, it was a long process, and in the meantime she married again, to John Joseph Orange, but by 1882 she owned two blocks on Freestone Creek, a total of 105 acres. Mary died in 1900, aged 68 years.

Naturally not all emigrants desired to pursue their careers on the land; thousands emigrated from Cornwall to escape the worn out or poor-paying mines there; between 1836-86 12,900 migrants left Cornwall, 8 per cent of the county's population. A high proportion made their way to Australia where it was natural for them to make use of their in-bred knowledge; some turned to well-sinking, an essential ingredient to life in the outback – in 1838 one Cornish emigrant, Joseph Pedlar, wrote home to say that he was earning £10-12 per month sinking wells.[24] Another, John Paull, from Goonvrea, St Agnes, wrote to his father, Erasmus:[25]

I have been working at well sinking and I have got £4 and sometimes £5 per week. Sometimes I have cut grass and have got £1 per day and if I did not get more than 5 shillings per day I count it slight. Now I am working at bricklaying and stone building and I have done very well. I believe our family have done as well as any that have come out here. Fat pork is 9d per pound and fresh pork is 14d per pound but I have nine pigs – two large and seven small ones. I have bought some land and built a house which cost me £100, This is what I saved in my first year.

In 1841, rich specimens of silver-lead ore, galena, were found by two Cornishmen, Thomas and Hutchins, near Adelaide at Glen Osmond, and the Wheal Gawler mine was started.[26] The copper mines at Kapunda and Burra Burra (South Australia) attracted more miners, earning 3s 6d for every £1 worth of ore raised. Emigration agents, particularly in Devon and Cornwall, were harassed to send more and more migrants out from the mining areas of those counties – in 1854, Henry Ayers of the South Australian Mining Association offered James Wilcocks, the official Emigration Agent in Plymouth, a personal bounty of £2 per head for up to 500 Cornish miners,[27] so desperate were they for more men. In the 1860s the Moonta Mines were opened up, Yelta, Wallaroo, Kadina – an area on South Australia's Yorke Peninsula known to this day as Australia's 'Little Cornwall'.[28]

> Twas Grannie who lived near the old Burra Mine
> And we often went up on a Sunday to dine
> At Redruth*, where Grannie lived. Grannie would tell
> Us stories of Cornwall when she was a 'gel',
> Oh, not in the world was a country so fine
> As Cornwall.[29]

Henry Hancock, born at Horrabridge (Devon) in 1836, sailed to Australia in 1859; he was appointed assayer to the Moonta Mining Company and later became superintendent of the Moonta Mine. Known as the 'Captain', he apparently sacked all the existing staff and appointed as managers a group of Cornishmen – M. Deeble, William and James Datson, J. Barkla and C. Mitchell. It is said that he worked from a pulpit nine feet high – to avoid his papers being overlooked, and had 15 speaking tubes into his office so that he could be in direct contact with different departments.[30]

A good living could be made in the towns and cities too, and by shrewd investment and good judgement not a few fortunes were made there. Richard Harding Butler, for example, the third son in a family of eight at Pensford (now Avon) never even considered becoming a farmer – his eldest brother, Henry, automatically assumed the tenancy of the family farm. Richard was good with figures, so launched himself into a financial career by becoming a clerk in the Dorset and Wells Bank in Glastonbury (Somerset).[31]

Richard was a keen tennis player, and regularly cycled off to West Bradley, a small village three or four miles out of the town to play; there he met Maud Austin of Baltonsborough and they became unofficially engaged. But their liaison was frowned upon by Maud's father because Richard 'owned no land', and in exasperation Richard decided to emigrate – hoping to establish himself in Australia sufficiently to claim his fiancée's hand.

Luckily all worked according to plan – he obtained a post at the Bank

*Redruth, South Australia.

Unveiling the plaque, in 1928, on the cottage at Charlton Mackrell where Charles Summers was born on 1825. (By courtesy of Woodspring Museum).

of Australia in Sydney and after only two years felt secure and confident enough to return and seek Mr Austin's permission to marry his daughter. His proposal accepted by both parties, he and Maud were married in St Dunstan's Church, Baltonsborough, in January 1886.[32]

The couple went back to Australia and settled in Ashfield, near Sydney, where Richard formed a firm of accountants. Other members of the family, fired by Richard's spirit, joined them – including one of Richard's younger brothers, Walter, who became one of the leading architects in Victoria.[33]

In May 1928 a small memorial tablet was unveiled on a very unprepossessing cottage in the village of Charlton Mackrell (Somerset), not far from Baltonsborough and West Bradley; the little cottage was the birthplace of Charles Summers. At the ceremony, the rector, the Reverend L. A. Bellhouse, said – and it was true – that 'the memory of

167

Charles Summers, one who ought to be remembered, had practically died out'.[34] Charles was born on 27 July 1825; his father, George, came of a family of masons, but 'owing to the peculiarities [of George], [Charles] did not receive the advantages of education which he should have been in a position to receive....he had to support his family at a time when he should have been free to train himself for his ultimate occupation'.[35] Charles' father was a drunkard, so 'the boy' was sent out to work from a very early age.

After working for a time on the building of the Union Workhouse in Wells (Somerset), the father and son heard of Brunel's need for labourers in constructing the railway line to Weston-super-Mare;[36] they moved to the fast-growing town and remained after the opening of the

Charles Summers (1827-78), born at Charlton Mackrell (Somerset); from The Australian Sketcher, *15 February 1879.*

railway in 1841, there being much work for masons. Charles' interest and skill in carving both stone and wood were noticed by Henry Weekes' foreman, when Charles was employed to help set up a monument for the parish church in Weston, and in 1846 he went to London to work in Weekes' studio as a polisher.

Every night Charles practised modelling and in December 1848 he was admitted as a student in the Royal Academy Schools; he exhibited in the Academy's Summer Exhibition in 1849, winning a silver medal for a model from the Antique – a relief of *'Silenus and the Infant Bacchus'*.[37] He continued to exhibit annually until 1853; but in the meantime he got married, to Augustine Amiot, on 9 June 1851, and became progressively ill with consumption, aggravated by overwork and the London atmosphere. Although he had won a scholarship to study in Rome, he chose instead to follow his father and brothers by emigrating to Australia; he hoped that the sea voyage would do him good, and he prefered to wait 'until his own taste was sufficiently matured to appreciate the beauties of Roman Fine Art'.

Charles sailed for Melbourne in 1852, in the *Hope*, leaving his wife behind until he could get established. His health was restored by the trip and he arrived fighting fit. His first task was to get a house and the only way he could afford one was to build his own – he purchased a piece of land in Docker Street, Richmond, and set to work.[38]

Determined to make out, he then went off to join his brothers in the goldfields at Tarnagulla. He laboured there conscientiously for six months until he saw an advertisement for modellers for the new Houses of Parliament building in Melbourne – he quickly returned. Ironically, just a week after he sold his gold claim, the buyers struck it very rich.

Captain Pasley, the Chief Commissioner of Public Works in Melbourne, liked the samples of Charles' work and he was placed in charge of the sculpture work in the Legislative Council, completed in 1856. Over the following decade, Charles in his studio in Collins Street became a central figure in artistic circles in Victoria; he arranged annual art exhibitions and was a founder of the Victorian Society of Fine Arts in 1856, he was a member of the commission of inquiry into the promotion of the fine arts in Victoria and was made chairman of a board of examiners testing drawing instructors for schools.[39]

Having completed his work for the Government, Charles began to undertake a variety of commissions: a Faun for the Melbourne Public Library, a statue of Shakespeare, a group for the Australian Mutual

169

Provident Society, reliefs for the Bank of New South Wales, and portraits, busts and medallions of local notables such as Charles Sturt, Sir Charles Darling, Sir Redmond Barry and J.P.Fawkner. His finest achievement and enduring monument to his skill is the colossal bronze group of Burke and Wills, the heroic explorers of central Australia who died at Coopers Creek in 1861 (of whom, more later). The whole of Australia was rocked by their fate, and a public fund for a monument was opened; Charles won the competition for its commission.[40]

He modelled the group, 13 feet high, in plaster. To cast it in bronze, a reverberatory furnace was erected, but his first effort, cast in two pieces, was scrapped because he could not bear to see his work joined in any way. The second and satisfactory casting was the largest attempted in the southern hemisphere. Around the granite plinth of the monument, Charles planned four reliefs, illustrating particular events during the expedition; in order to achieve the greatest accuracy, he spent six weeks in the bush modelling aborigines from life. On 21 April 1865 the great monument was unveiled and Charles received £4,000 and much acclaim.[41] Now ready for Rome, Charles decided to return to Europe; he sailed for England in May 1867 on the *True Briton*.[42]

Relief sculpture of The Good Samaritan, by Charles Summers, c1868-9, on the Old Hospital, Weston-super-Mare (Avon).

William and Mary (née Lakey) Dyer, from farm labouring families, emigrants from Ilfracombe (Devon) to Pine Hill (Queensland) in the 1880s; they purchased cattle and a block of land, Horwood Farm, where their descendants continue farming to this day. (By courtesy of Miss Q.Dyer, Teignmouth).

More typical of the later emigrants from the West Country were William and Mary Dyer (née Lakey); both from North Devon labouring families, they were married at Instow (Devon) in 1881 and left for Australia soon after their wedding.[43] William Dyer found work on the Central Queensland Railway at Pine Hill, but with his eye always on a farm of his own he was among the first selectors on the land to the west opened up by the extension of the railway. For a time he continued with his job on the line, going up to his block whenever he could to build a house. He purchased some cattle from Bogantungan but his land was still unfenced and they persistently returned home; just as persistently he brought them back again.[44]

When the house was ready he took his family to live there, calling the block Horwood Farm, after a place in Devon where he had worked. At first he tried to carry out all he had learnt at home, even to cutting the natural grass with a scythe and making a haystack; apparently the seasons were good and the haystack was never used. The Dyers had eight children, and all four sons settled in the district; Frank took over the original Horwood estate, adding neighbouring blocks as they became available. 100 years later, William Dyer's farm has grown to 60,000 acres, and is stocked with pedigree Herefords.[45]

9 GOLD FEVER

When first I left Old England's shore
Such yarns as we were told,
As how folks in Australia
Could pick up lumps of gold.
So, when we got to Melbourne town,
We were ready soon to slip
And get even with the captain -
All hands scuttled from the ship.[1]

At the height of the gold rush ships' captains had to bribe their crews not to desert as soon as the vessel docked; many a ship lay abandoned, unable to muster a crew to sail home; clergy left their churches, doctors their practises and lawyers their offices. All sorts of people were drawn by the irresistable urge to get rich quick – the aristocracy, joked the old-timers, dug for gold with their gloves on. Gold was a great leveller, and gold, it is said, brought democracy to Australia.

The first significant gold strike hit the headlines in May 1851, it was at Lewis Ponds Creek, Yorke's Corner near Bathurst, in New South Wales,[2] but far richer fields quickly became bonanzas: particularly Buninyong near Ballarat and Castlemaine near Bendigo, both in Victoria; by the end of the year the news had spread across the world, and it was via Melbourne, Victoria's major port, that most of the immigrants made their way to the gold diggings. Over the following decade, the population of Australia nearly trebled, but the population of Victoria increased more than 500 per cent.[3]

An attempt was made to control the flood, and to bring some benefit to Government coffers, by imposing a licence fee, £1 10s per month – payable in advance. The licences were issued on the spot, but to obtain one, it was necessary to present a certificate from one's employer, stating that one had been formally discharged;[4] needless-to-say, there was much evasion.

Strangely enough, the gold rushes did not draw that many Cornish miners away from the copper mines – the Cornish were professional deep-miners, not given to scratching the surface or panning for alluvial ore,[5] but fortune hunters arrived from every other corner, including unexpected hordes from China. By 1852 there were 50,000 diggers along the Bendigo Creek; the landscape dotted with tents and pock-marked by shallow holes – prices rocketed and 'anyone who had a team of horses or bullocks then made a fortune'.[6] £100 a ton was paid for the mere carriage of flour to Bendigo, and flour worth £25 in Melbourne was sold on the goldfield for £200.

On 4 September 1851 the *North Devon Journal*, not reknowned for its international interests, reported 'Gold fever in Australia' and quoted the *Sydney Morning Herald*:[7]

> scores have rushed from their homes provided with a blanket, a 'damper' and a pick or grubbing hoe, full of hope that a day or two's labour would fill their pockets with the precious metal.

The news fired the imagination of an unlikely group of local business men – William Avery, a draper, John Edger a grocer and Thomas King, an ironmonger – to form the North Devon Shipping Company with the aim of building a vessel to carry emigrants from North Devon to the goldfields.[8] They set to work quickly and commissioned John Westacott's yard in Barnstaple to build a clipper of 400 tons or so – one of the largest ships yet built on the River Taw. By 3 June 1852 she was ready to be launched and was named *Lady Ebrington*, after Georgina, the wife of the Liberal candidate for Barnstaple.

Just three weeks later, the *North Devon Journal* carried the following advertisment:[9]

Australia Gold Regions
Emigration to Port Philip.
Parties desirous of proceeding with the greatest possible despatch will find a particularly favourable opportunity in the sailing of the North Devon Shipping Company's New and Splendid Clipper-built ship
Lady Ebrington
700 tons burthen, A1, Fourteen years at Lloyds.
G.Harris, Commander.
....she will be despatched on 15 August 1852 and as two-thirds of her complement are already engaged immediate application should be made for the remaining berths.

The departure of the Lady Ebrington *from Barnstaple;* Illustrated London News, *28 August 1852.*

When the *Lady Ebrington* finally sailed in October, it is surprising that only 129 out of an anticipated 150 berths had been filled, and there could have been room for even more – perhaps the problem was her size, for much larger vessels, up to 1,000 tons and presumably that much more stable, were already sailing to Australia from the more established emigration ports.

Passengers boarded the *Lady Ebrington* at Barnstaple and Appledore and on the whole they were impressed by what they found – one assisted emigrant from Ilfracombe, Charles Jenkins, wrote to his sister in glowing terms telling her how he got a pint of porter every day, preserved milk for the baby, and 'pork three times a week, preserved meat and plum pudding four days, beef one'.[10]

The voyage took 107 days; soon after his arrival a young farmer, Mr Southcombe, wrote home:[11]

> I cannot withstand the temptation of the diggings. I have made up a strong and pretty wealthy party, and we start to the Forrest

Creek diggings on Thursday morning....We have made out a proper agreement, are bound together for three months, and all have resolved not to take a drop of beer, wine or spirits for that time; and should it prove successful, we intend to stay there for twelve months. Steady men are making their fortunes very fast, but drunkards should not come here.

We steered our course for Geelong Town,
Then north-west to Ballarat,
Where some of us got mighty thin,
And some got sleek and fat.
Some tried their luck at Bendigo,
And some at Fiery Creek;
I made a fortune in a day
And spent it in a week.[12]

The gold seekers were generally adventurous, single and young; although they might afford their fares to Melbourne, many found themselves unable to pay the inflated prices demanded on arrival for

Off to the diggings at Bathurst; all manner of people left their employment and homes to seek a fortune in the goldfields. Illustrated London News, *15 November 1851.*

rent, food and transport; simply getting themselves and their luggage ashore could cost as much as the fare from England. A 'Canvas Town' of makeshift shelters grew up on the edge of Melbourne. Governor La Trobe commented:

> It is evident that amongst the newcomers not one in ten is prepared to encounter the crush and labour of the Gold Fields, and that the great majority are probably totally unfitted and unsuited by previous habits, occupation or temperament to surmount the difficulties which must beset them in becoming colonists at the present time.[13]

Some emigrants to the goldfields, like Frank Allen from Baltonsborough (Somerset), just disappeared; his family never heard of him again[14]. Of the 188 emigrants who left Jersey on the *Evening Star* in 1854, only a handful disembarked at Semaphore, South Australia, and the majority pressed on to Melbourne – little is known of their enterprise but there is no doubt that they were encouraged by the tales of wealth and fortune on the goldfields.[15] Others were able to send money home and there were some notable success stories; John Day and Thomas Harris returned home, in 1855, to Weare Giffard (Devon) after only 14 months away and rang the church bells to announce that they had found one of the largest nuggets yet discovered in Australia – it weighed 85 pounds and was said to be worth more than £4,000;[16] Noah Symons and Abel Stoyle, cousins, also from North Devon, were away for five years – having made their fortunes at the diggings they came home in style as first-class passengers on a steamer, with a week's holiday at Cape Town on the way; they presented their amazed fathers with £100 apiece, and then strolled into a Barnstaple bank to deposit £1,000 each;[17] Cornish emigrants returned to their home ports, Penzance and Falmouth, to show off their finds – in April 1852 70,000 ounces of gold, worth £25,000, were landed at Penzance alone and the following year a 'goldfields display' was exhibited in Truro and Falmouth.[18]

Not all emigrants in the 1850s, though, were lured by the glitter of gold; for some the hard living miners became a target for a different kind of zeal. The first ever religious service at Bendigo was taken by a Cornishman, James Jeffery, and another Cornish preacher, William Moyle, roamed the goldfields – first to Bendigo and later, in 1853, to Ballarat – he combined preaching with a little prospecting of his own but his gold-seeking efforts were dogged by ill-luck; it was said of him: 'Good Father Moyle was always richer in grace than in gold....'.[19]

Isaac Harding had made his name as a forceful Wesleyan preacher around the Mendip villages near his home at Marksbury (now Avon); as early as 1838 he had expressed a wish to 'preach among the neglected and benighted thousands of our antipodes', but it was not until 1853 that he finally went, taking with him his seven year old daughter and his wife, Eliza, who gave birth to a second daughter at Cape Town on the way out. While stationed in Melbourne, Isaac visited the goldfields at Ballarat and Bendigo thinking nothing of riding a hundred miles from home to distribute books and pamphlets and to preach to tiny communities in the back-of-beyond. His obituary in the Melbourne *Spectator* reported that 'traditions still linger of the great space of country over which he rode in a day'.[20]

Digging for gold was certainly a lottery, and some, like 'Crosbie' in *His Natural Life*,[21] preferred a safer, if steadier, path to riches on the goldfields:

> When half the world is mad upon digging, no one thinks of such slow-going trades as those of the butcher and baker. If you get ten ounces of gold a week, and can't buy bread, what's the good of your money? Wouldn't you give five ounces for a loaf?

Licences to dig for gold were issued by Commissioner John Hardy in the Bathurst Gold District; evasion was common, note the gold seekers hiding behind a rock, and others making off up the hill.

Crosbie's General Store was well placed and his fortune assured for the sake of the novel – in reality even the catering trade on the diggings was fraught with problems: George Rowe was, in many ways, an unlikely fortune-hunting emigrant; he was an artist of some repute, and middle-aged by the time of the gold rush. He was born (in 1796) and brought up in Exeter, the son of a builder and auctioneer, Joseph Rowe. As a young man George achieved some fame for his lithographed views of Devon, Cornwall and Somerset before moving to Cheltenham in 1832.[22] There he practised as a lithographic printer and also as an 'Artist and Drawing Master', aided in his Academy first by his wife, Philippa (née Curtis) and later by his daughter Phillipa. Although something of a

Panning for alluvial gold was facilitated by the 'cradle', the box-like object on the left, which was rocked to and fro to reveal, one hoped, grains of gold caught on a sieve.

radical, George Rowe joined the establishment by accepting an invitation to become one of the Town Commissioners, and, for a two year term, High Bailiff; he had a finger in many pies, including the local paper, the Pump Room, and speculative building; but the paper became involved in a series of libel actions, the theatrical performances in the Pump Room attracted poor audiences, and his building speculations were over-stretched.[23] So in 1852, prompted by despair at his situation in Cheltenham, and by a desire to recoup his losses in order to support his family, he decided to make for the goldfields. Such was his financial plight, that he even had to borrow to pay his fare[24] A letter written to his wife a couple of days before his departure suggests that creditors could have been on his tail:[25]

> I had a letter from Boodle [the man who lent him money for the fare] this morning in which he says all is quiet....I do not fear but all is right, they will not suspect anything until Wednesday when I hope to be far away on the open sea...

Tears flooded into his eyes as he said his last good-byes and wrote: 'What I am doing is I feel for our mutual good and I must keep up a good heart'. On 30 June 1852 he sailed from London as a cabin passenger on the ship *Panama*.[26] George was lucky to win the respect of the ship's captain, Captain Thomas, to whom he presented two watercolours of Tenerife and on arrival at Port Phillip, Thomas allowed him to live on board ship for some weeks, and even paid him 20 shillings a day to help unload the ship's cargo, the rest of the crew having run off to the goldfields.[27]

George stayed in Port Phillip to await the arrival of his eldest son, George Curtis Rowe, who was to follow him to Australia as soon as possible; on his arrival a few weeks later, father and son took up residence in a tent on Lehard's Beach, at Hobson's Bay, near Melbourne until 14 December, when they finally set out for the goldfields in the company of ten others, including the ship's doctor from the *Panama*, Dr Hoyle.[28]

George and his party headed for the Castlemaine diggings, 70 miles north of Melbourne; they pitched their tent at Campbell's Creek and began to sink a hole in search of 'the yellow dust that we have come so many thousands of miles to look for'. Poor old George, though, went down with dysentry and was confined to his tent for a fortnight. George junior and Dr Hoyle persevered. They had little luck and scarcely covered their living expenses.

It was at this point that George senior opted out and decided to try catering for the miners instead. He went into partnership with Samuel Isaacs, with whom he had shared a cabin on the *Panama;* together they purchased tea, coffee and sugar from Melbourne and resold them at a profit to the diggers. The success of the venture encouraged George to set up a more ambitious 'Refreshment Tent', where tea, coffee and lemonade could be sold and with the dry season approaching he thought that the best place to operate it would be at Bendigo, another 30 miles north.[29]

So, George and his son moved camp and established their 'eating and coffee house' in partnership with a Mr Robertson, 'in a very popular spot of the diggings near the busiest place and was surrounded with thousands of tents'.[30] Unfortunately their timing could not have been worse, for 'just a few days before we were ready to open news came of the discovery of a new gold field being found at McIvor and the whole

The Post Office and provisions tents at Forest Creek; from Rev.T.Braim's 'New Homes...', 1887.

population took flight leaving poor [us] with a nice building fitted up comfortably and every requisite towards making money with hardly a nickel in my pocket'. They carried on the business for some time, but found that they could not make a living. 'One day', wrote George to his wife, 'I had but 6s 2d left, Mr Robertson and George had nothing, so I turned to my own profession, painted a few pictures not dreaming that I should be at all successful, but I was and soon got a few pounds together'.[31]

By July 1853, he was able to write with some optimism to his wife:

> Now have in hand one drawing at 5 guineas and four at 2 guineas and about twenty at a guinea – all bespoke – so that in my next I hope to be able to enclose you some cash....at present I paint two one guinea drawings per day...[George] is engaged and has sung for the past week at the large concert room [in fact a large tent] elegantly fitted up, called the 'Crystal Palace'. He is to have a guinea per night....The room is crowded every night; the Magistrate and the Gold Commissioners were there last night and expressed themselves highly delighted....

Other letters home vividly describe life around the goldfields:[32]

> You entertain very erroneous ideas about the diggings. They are become more respectable and safe than a town in the colony. When I tell you that within a few tents of us we had a Wesleyan Chapel on one side and on the other a Church...All around are tents with men with wives and families, evidently very respectable people – very neat and well and on Sunday go to Church or Chapel....

By the end of August 1853, only ten months after his arrival in Australia, he was able to send £50 home to his wife.

> Last week a Wedding [a Digger's Wedding] in the flat just below us. The Bride's trousseau cost £150 – a friend at a store near us supplied the things. After the marriage ceremony the gay party went for a ride in a nice vehicle and four horses decorated with white flowers – there was a large party at the father of the Bride's tent in the evening. Plenty of good things were provided and wines of all description flowed liberally. In the midst of the revelry the Bridegroom slipped off with his Bride to his own tent and her future home. It is not the fashion here for the happy pair to spend the honeymoon on tour.....

Last Sunday being Xmas Day the Doct.Hoyle and Clint dined
with us when we had roast Veal and ham with green peas and
Lobsters and took our Barkly & Perkins, real bottle porter from
London – enjoyed our Wine and Walnuts after dinner.....all I
wear now is a pair of canvas trousers and a Shirt and pr. of Shoes. I
like this warm weather and the evenings are delicious.

George was painting busily, most of his work commissioned by fellow
diggers, views of the diggings and portraits. He explained his success by
the fact that most of his fellow settlers 'have recently left their homes and
their country, all have someone to whom they are attached and they wish
to send them some token of recollection, what better than a view of their

Assistant-commissioner receiving gold for escort to Melbourne; Illustrated
London News, *22 January 1853.*

residence, or a sketch of themselves; almost all I have painted are to be sent to England or America'. He also continued to sell drinks and food from his tent, branching out into tobacco, biscuits, milk, vegetables and eggs.

George's pictures earned him an important place among Australia's goldfield artists and his last years in the country were marked by a considerable degree of public recognition. In 1857, 50 of his water colours of the Bendigo and Castlemaine diggings were made the subject of an Art Union at Bendigo, in which 420 subscribers each paid £1 to gain the chance of winning one of his paintings.[33] The *Melbourne Argus* reported that:[34]

> Mr Rowe possesses a bold and graphic pencil, and has produced some exceedingly good sketches of places which will never fail to be interesting to thousands of persons in this colony for many years to come. Nearly all his drawings have a degree of merit, but we are especially attracted. amongst others, by *Loddon Plains from Mount Alexander, Sailors Gully with Mount Korong in the Distance, The Summit of Mount Alexander*, the large *View of Sandhurst, Mount Blackwood* and several others which we recommend readers to inspect for themselves.

George returned to England in about 1859, leaving George junior, and two younger sons who had joined them later, in Australia; he settled in Exeter. In 1862 he was awarded a medal for a series of paintings exhibited in the Mining, Quarrying and Metallurgy Section of the London International Exhibition for 'faithful and beautiful delineation of the country, workings, and other relations of the gold fields' – several of these pictures are now in the Mitchell Library, Sydney, the National Library, and the Bendigo Art Gallery. He died at Heavitree, Exeter, on 2 September 1864.[35]

By the mid 1850s it was becoming increasingly difficult to make that elusive fortune; prospecting miners hopped from one site to another, always hopeful – but the superficial deposits had all but been cleared and deeper mines were needed to reach remaining ores, requiring engineering skill and heavy equipment. The miners frustration, and their annoyance at having to pay the 30 shillings a month licence fee, bubbled over in November 1854, when 800 of them refused to pay up; the 2nd. South Somersetshire Regiment,[36] on their second term of duty in the colony, were called to sort things out and marched in to face the miners barricaded behind the Eureka Stockade at dawn on 3 December – an event that has been glamourised into Australian folklore and legend. 50 miners were killed or wounded, half a dozen soldiers died and the uprising was crushed, but the miners had won the moral victory and soon afterwards the licence fee was abolished, to be replaced by an export duty of 2s/6d an ounce.[37]

The hordes that had once swarmed around the goldfields began to disperse, back home, or to more regular settlements within Australia – the hastily built taverns and hotels of the gold rush camps were abandoned to decay into ghost towns. But the State of Victoria had prospered, and Melbourne had, in the space of a few years, been able to adorn herself with every symbol of material progress.

Gold changed Australia; if it brought democracy, it also helped to seal the end of transportation. Back in England the government could no longer consider New South Wales to be a prison Gulag when thousands of Englishmen were queueing up to pay their own fares to get there. The horror of the threat of transportation had disappeared and over the following years the number of convicts transported steadily declined until 1867 when the last transport ship left England.

They'll charge you seven shillings for a pint of mouldy peas,
Six and ninepence-farthing for a pound of rotten cheese.
Of going a gold digging, friends, I think I've had my full,
May the devil take Australia, I'll live with Old John Bull.[38]

10   THE EXPLORERS

The sheer size of the Australian land mass and the inhospitality of the interior rendered exploration a slow and hazardous business. In the early days there was a constant fear that the French might suddenly step in and claim a hunk of the continent for themselves, so efforts were made to chart the coast and to note sheltered havens for future settlement. Norfolk Island was speedily annexed by Governor Phillip, followed by Van Dieman's Land as a secondary penal camp and then Port Phillip.

One of the first people to explore inland from Moreton Bay penal settlement was Major Edmund Lockyer[1], who in 1825 was sent in a small cutter, the *Mermaid*, to follow the Brisbane River. Lockyer was from Plymouth (Devon); his father, Thomas, was a successful merchant and sailmaker – he built Wembury House in the village of Wembury (six miles east of Plymouth) – Edmund was baptised in St Andrew's Church, Plymouth on 21 January 1784; he joined the army and in 1824 his regiment, the 57th Regiment of Foot, 'the Diehards', was ordered to New South Wales. He sailed from Portsmouth on the *Royal Charlotte*, with his wife, Sarah, née Morris (also from Plymouth), and family.[2]

Lockyer's expedition ably negotiated the Brisbane River venturing 120 miles or so upstream and he reported back most favourably on the potential of the area for future development.

Edmund Lockyer had only been back in Sydney for a month when Governor Darling put him in command of another expedition, this time to King George Sound. The Governor had received a secret communication from Earl Bathurst, the Secretary of State at the Colonial Office in London, concerning the possible intentions of the French regarding Western Australia and the instruction to establish a claim there for the British crown;[3] at that time there was no settlement in Western Australia, nor recognised sovereignty over more than a third of the continent. Captain Joseph Wakefield was chosen to lead a small detachment from the 39th Regiment of the Dorsetshires, on tour of duty in the colony, to accompany Lockyer and to guard the 23 convicts, selected for their skills useful to the proposed settlement, who went too.

They sailed from Sydney on 9 November 1826 in the brig *Amity;* the party also included Lockyer's son, Edmund junior, as storekeeper, a surgeon, Isaac Nind, and a gardener, ex-convict John Browne; they carried stores to last six months and livestock – hens, pigs and sheep. Unfortunately the voyagers hit foul weather and were forced to go south of Van Dieman's Land – they put in to Hobart Town for a short respite. At last, on Christmas Day 1826 they reached King George Sound; they found a good harbour, but were disappointed by the poor quality of the soil. Soon after their arrival one of the convicts was speared by a native when collecting water, but they subsequently discovered that the natives themselves had been cruelly treated by whalers using the harbour for shelter, so Lockyer insisted there should be no retribution.

The stores were unloaded and a little settlement gradually emerged – tents, huts, and the first efforts at cultivated ground. On 21 January 1827, Lockyer's forty-third birthday, the Colours were hoisted on the flagstaff, a 21 gun salute fired and Major Lockyer formally took possession of the western third of Australia for the British Crown. He recorded in his journal:[4]

> An extra allowance of flour with raisons and suet was ordered on the occasion to be issued to the troops and convicts. A number of the natives having come to the settlement in the morning, the same was handed on purpose to give them a feast. About three hundredweight was taken of capital fish. The day proved fine, and the whole went off well.

Lockyer named the settlement 'Frederickstown', in honour of His Royal Highness the Duke of York, Frederick Augustus, (the name was later changed to Albany) and just three days later the *Amity* returned to Sydney, leaving the convict settlers and soldiers under Lockyer to fare as best they could.

On 3 April, Lockyer left too, aboard the *Success,* with Captain James Stirling, who had put in to the harbour fresh from his exploration of the Swan River, and Captain Wakefield was left in command of Frederickstown.

Six years later, when Sir Richard Spencer arrived as the Government Resident of Albany, he found just 17 civilians, a few soldiers, dilapidated buildings and a moribund economy; Sir Richard and his

Portrait of Sir Richard Spencer, 1779-1839; Government Resident of Albany, Western Australia from 1833-39. (Courtesy of the Lyme Regis Museum, Mr A.Brown)

family injected new life by initiating a programme of public works, native welfare, a police force and surveys of the surrounding territory. As Captain Spencer, Sir Richard had enjoyed a distinguished and gallant naval career, serving under Nelson; in 1817 he retired on half-pay to Lyme Regis (Dorset) where he farmed with his wife Ann, daughter of Mrs Liddon, who owned the manor of Charmouth, nearby.[5] The Spencers sailed for Australia well equipped for their pioneering venture,

No.6 Cobb Road, Lyme Regis, the family home of Richard and Ann Spencer.

with the storeship *Buffalo* chock-a-block with plants, fruit trees, livestock, farm implements, stores and servants; on arrival they bought Strawberry Hill, and to its six cleared acres they quickly added 1,400 virgin acres, ripe for improvement.[6] The house they built, Old Farm, Strawberry Hill survives and is now owned and cared for by the Australian National Trust.

Edmund Lockyer, back in Sydney, decided to settle permanently in Australia; he retired from the army and built a house called Ermington near Parramatta. News of his success reached England and he was rewarded in his home town by being elected a Freeman of the Borough of Plymouth. In 1835 he was granted 2,560 acres of land near Goulburn, south of Sydney, in recognition of his achievements; he named the area Lockyersleigh.

Charles Sturt, another officer of the 39th Regiment, set off on his first expedition, encouraged by Governor Darling, on 10 November 1828. Sturt had been born in India in 1795, but his parents were from Dorset families of long-standing.[7] Sturt hoped for the honour of discovering the great inland sea which was presumed to lie somewhere in the middle of the continent – so many rivers appeared to head that way. Together with an experienced explorer, Hamilton Hume, three soldiers and eight convicts, he fought his way through the marshes of the Upper Macquarie River, previously thought impenetrable. The season was abominable, the country blasted by drought and searing heat. On 2 February they came suddenly on 'a noble river' flowing west, which Sturt named the Darling; unhappily its waters were undrinkable at that point because of salt springs.[8]

After a journey of more than 1,200 miles through unknown country they returned to Sydney, if anything the more convinced about the existence of an inland sea. Athough he was ill, Sturt completed a report on the journey and was scrupulous in recommending the convicts in his party for such indulgences as the colonial government could grant.

After a few months he was off again; this time up the Murrumbidgee in a whale boat. He found and named the Murray River, in honour of Sir George Murray, Secretary of State for the Colonies. Sturt and his party followed the river until it entered another larger stream flowing in from the north; Sturt was convinced that this was the Darling and they continued on down to its sandy channel to the sea. Depressed and dismayed by failing to find either an effective inland waterway or the ship which Governor Darling had promised to send from Sydney, Sturt

Captain Sir Charles Sturt of the 39th Regiment, the Dorsetshires.

now faced the appalling prospect of rowing more than 900 miles upstream against a strong current, with his men already weary and food in short supply.[9]

They made it, but Sturt's health was wrecked, to say nothing of that of his men, and he was forced to return to England and had to leave the Regiment. On the voyage his eyesight, which had been failing, broke down completely, leaving him totally blind. While undergoing crude but moderately successful treatment for his condition he published an account of his two journeys.

In 1835 Sturt sailed for New South Wales again, with his wife,

Charlotte née Green, to take up his land grant - 5,000 acres at Ginninderra (near Canberra). In spite of such a promising start, things went badly wrong; he got mixed up with a rather crazy venture for overlanding cattle to South Australia, then with a dodgy land transaction and hence into financial difficulties. Incredibly he managed to muster support for yet another exploration and in August 1844 left Adelaide with 15 men, six drays, a boat and 200 sheep still searching for the inland sea.[10]

This time they followed the Murray River to its junction with the Darling, then on up the Darling. For six sweltering summer months they were trapped at a waterhole, surrounded by impassable country; Sturt's second-in-command, James Poole, died of scurvy. In July they were released by heavy rain. They staggered about the Cooper's Creek and the Murray area, continually battling with outbreaks of scurvy until January 1846 when they arrived back in Adelaide.

Sturt's sight began to fail again and in order to secure some sort of future for his children he decided to return to England – he spent his last years in Cheltenham (Gloucestershire).[11]

Meanwhile other officers of the 39th Regiment, not content with mooching about guarding their convict charges, began to make their presence felt. Captain Walpole succeeded in rounding up a gang of convicts who had broken out and were terrorising the Bathurst district.[12] Captain J.D.Forbes, together with Lieutenant Maule, a Royal Navy doctor and three soldiers gained valuable experience exploring uncharted country in the Central Tableland in 1830, and a couple of years later he put his knowledge to good use when he was sent out with a team of mounted police to round up some bushrangers. Journals of both exploits survive in the Dorset Military Museum, Dorchester.[13]

A well-earned and peaceful retirement back in the pleasant suburbs of a provincial English town was a rare thing for Australia's early explorers; more likely their corpse, shrivelled like a prune, lay deserted and lost in a wasteland. Edmund Besley Court Kennedy, from Guernsey, attempted to cross the Cape York peninsula from Rockingham Bay with his aboriginal companion, Jackey Jackey, in 1848 – he was speared and killed by natives.[14] Ernest Giles' assistant, a man named Conn, was not only killed but partially eaten by natives near Cooktown, Queensland,[15] and Giles himself, from a middle class Bristol family, only just survived his five explorations through Western and Central Australia in the

1870s.[16] Burke and Wills died of exhaustion on their return journey having completed the first crossing of the continent from south to north.

William Wills was a Devon lad; he was born in Totnes on 5 January 1834, the son of the local surgeon, also William, and Sarah, the youngest daughter of William Calley, an 'elderly and respected inhabitant'.[17] He was educated at Ashburton Grammar School until the age of 16 when he began to study medicine in his father's surgery.

In 1852 William's father quite suddenly applied to be taken on as a medical officer on an emigrant ship (a bout of gold fever perhaps), and was engaged to join a vessel, sailing later that year; he arranged to take William and a younger son, Tom, with him.[18] There is no recorded explanation for the fact that it was only the two boys who went – they travelled from Dartmouth in one of Mr W.S.Lindsay's ships. William Wills senior postponed his voyage for another year.

William and Tom arrived in Melbourne and were initially employed as shepherds at Deniliquin, New South Wales; but when their father arrived, they moved to Ballarat to open a gold office. Dr Wills continued to practise medicine, when time allowed, and if he happened to be out, young William stepped in to attend the patients.[19]

In 1856, with the gold rush ebbing, William obtained an appointment under Mr F.Byerly to learn surveying. Interest in uncovering the enigma of the interior of the continent was at its height; Sturt's explorations had whetted the appetite for more and although a fist-full of adventurers scratched at the edges, what was really required was a trans-continental trip to answer the questions once and for all. To tackle such an epic journey responsibly was a major undertaking, and whilst Sydney and Melbourne vied with each other for the honour of launching an expedition, the cost was a matter of some concern.

The spur to activity was a generous donation of £1,000 towards the expedition from a prosperous Melbourne merchant, Ambrose Kyte, made anonymously and on condition that another £2,000 could be raised from public subscriptions within a year; the money came in and the Victorian Government, reluctant at first, now voted £6,000 to add to the total. An Exploration Committee was set up under the auspices of the Royal Society in Melbourne to superintend the arrangements.

The Committee was determined that the leader of the expedition should be from Victoria; the post was advertised in the Melbourne Press and 14 candidates applied; six were finally considered. One of them was a police superintendent from the Castlemaine district, Robert O'Hara

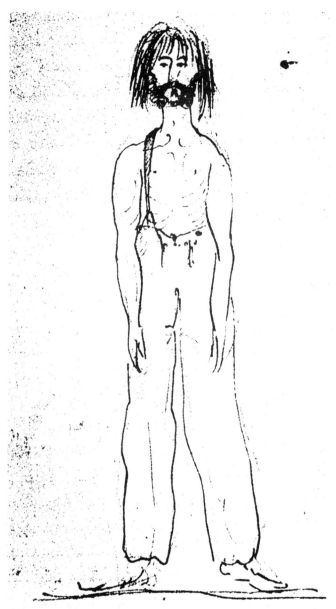

Self-portrait from the diary of Captain J.D.Forbes on his exploration of part of New South Wales in 1830; 'no shirt, no hat, no shoes. My long hair hanging down in a most melancholy looking state – I must try to draw myself for you'. (Courtesy of the Dorset Military Museum, Dorchester).

Burke, and eventually he was chosen by ten votes to five.[20]

Burke was a strange character, apparently in love with a popular singer of the time, Julia Matthews; a bank manager described him as a 'careless dare-devil sort of Irishman of very ordinary physique. He wore a long beard, over which he dribbled his saliva'.[21]

Second in command was George Landells who had been sent to India to acquire camels for the journey; he returned successfully with 24 of the beasts and a number of native drivers. Dr Ludwick Becker was appointed naturalist and artist, Dr Herman Beckler as botanist and medical adviser, and John King, a soldier from India, to help with the camels.

William Wills was appointed as surveyor – the man who would chart the expedition's route, he was recommended by Dr Neumayer, the meteorologist and an influential member of the Royal Society. Alan Moorehead, in his classic and detailed account of the whole expedition, *Cooper's Creek,* described Wills as 'one of Dickens' young heroes, fair-minded, compassionate, studious, eager to get on' with a passion for 'astronomy and meteorology and precise calculations and deductions .....his sense of direction was so good that he unravelled the mystery of the maze at Hampton Court in ten minutes'.[22]

Once the team had been selected public interest was fired; there was much to be done and seemingly endless preparations of the supplies required for a year or more away from civilisation. As the planned date of departure grew near, piles of equipment, scientific instruments, food and other supplies were laid out in Royal Park, Melbourne, until at last, on 21 August 1860, the waggons were loaded and the expedition given an official send-off by the Mayor amidst a huge crowd of well-wishers.

The waggon-train, camels and horses soon reached the northern boundary of the colony of Victoria, and it was about here that things began to go wrong. Burke fell out with his foreman, a man named Ferguson, and discharged him, but no sooner had he done so than George Landells began to sow dissention in the camp. By the time they arrived at Menindie, on the Darling River, the row had come to a head and after a violent scene Landells resigned, returning to Melbourne full of complaints against Burke. Luckily for Burke, Wills carefully recorded a full account of the events in a letter to Neumayer, and the Royal Society Committee was able to send its full approval of Burke's conduct and moreover to confirm Wills' promotion to second in command.[23]

Cartoon from the Melbourne Punch *entitled 'The Great Australian Exploration Race'.*

Leaving a depot and about half the party at Menindie, Burke pressed on. Wills wrote in a letter to a friend:[24]

> Riding on camels is a much more pleasant process than I had anticipated, and for my work I find it much better than riding on horseback. The saddles, as you are aware, are double, so I sit on the back portion behind the hump, and pack my instruments in front. I can thus ride on, keeping my journal and making calculations; and need only stop the camel when I want to take any bearings carefully; but the barometers can be read and registered without halting. The animals are very quiet and easily managed, much more so than the horses.

Burke sent another man, William Wright, back to bring up the remainder of the camels to Cooper's Creek immediately – incredibly, and presumably knowing that life or death might hang on his action – Wright failed to do what had been agreed. Meanwhile Burke's party arrived at the Creek on 11 November. In a letter to one of his sisters, Wills described the scene:[25]

> To give you an idea of Cooper's Creek, fancy extensive flat sandy plains, covered with herbs dried like hay, and imagine a creek or river, somewhat similar in appearance and size to the Dart above the Weir, winding its way through these flats, having its banks densely clothed with gum trees and other evergreens. So far there appears to be a considerable resemblance, but now for the difference. The water of Cooper's Creek is only a number of waterholes. In some places it entirely disappears, the water in flood-time spreading all over the flats, and forming no regular channel.

With no message nor sign of Wright and the camels coming up from Menindie, Burke was growing impatient; letters from the Committee in Melbourne had told him of a rival exploration, led by John Stuart, out of Adelaide and the pressure was on – newspapers fuelled 'the Great Australian Exploration Race'.[26] Burke determined to make a quick, light-weight, dash for the Gulf of Carpentaria, taking with him only Wills and two other men, John King and Charles Grey.

On Sunday 16 December they were off; they had one horse, six camels and three months' provisions. The remainder was left at Cooper's Creek as a base camp or depot, to await the long-expected arrival of Wright from Menindie; Burke's instructions to Brahe, the man left in charge at Cooper's Creek, scarcely considered the possibility that they might not return within three months.

In fact Burke was doing precisely what he had been advised not to do – he had split his expedition up into several disparate units with no formal lines of communication between them; he was travelling in mid-summer. His instructions to those left behind were hazy; and no one, except Wills, was travelling with him to record what they found – the expedition of discovery had become little more than a race.[27]

The journey to the Gulf covered 750 miles of uncharted country, stony desert, slippery swamps, hard-baked clay, blown and blowing sand and the ubiquitous flies; they frequently met surprisingly large groups of aborigines, 50 or 60 gathered together around a creek or waterhole. Wills wrote of one encounter:

197

A large tribe of blacks came pestering us to go to their camp and have a dance, which we declined. They were very troublesome, and nothing but the threat to shoot will keep them away; they are, however, easily frightened, and, although fine looking men, decidedly not of a warlike disposition. They show the greatest inclination to take whatever they can, but will run no unnecessary risk in doing so. They seldom carry any weapons, except a large shield and a kind of boomerang, which I believe they use for killing rats etc; sometimes, but very seldom, they have a large spear; reed spears seem to be quite unknown to them. They are undoubtedly a finer and better-looking race of men than the blacks on the Murray and Darling, and more peaceful...[28]

They spent Christmas Day 1860 at a pleasant oasis that they named Gray's Creek; strangely enough lack of water was no problem, in fact as they passed into the Tropics torrential downpours created a muddy morass, loathed by the camels and cursed by the men. One camel, Golah, had to be abandoned in a mud-filled creek, unable to haul itself out of the ooze.

On 30 January 1861, having got within 30 miles or so of the shores of the Gulf, Burke and Wills left Gray and King to look after the surviving camels, and with three days supplies they went on with the horse – Billy. Poor Billy got bogged down almost immediately and in the end even Burke and Wills, after all this trouble, could not break through the tangle of mangrove swamps to reach the open sea – they were forced to give up just a stone's throw from their goal. 'It would have been well', wrote Burke, 'to say that we reached the sea, but we could not obtain a view of the open ocean, although we made every endeavour to do so'.[29]

They rejoined Gray and King, and the one thought now in all their minds was how to reach the depot on Cooper's Creek before their rations ran out.

The mud and rain continued; it was so wet that Wills resorted to keeping his watch and field-book in a pack to try and keep them dry. To avoid the boggy flats, they travelled along the stony ridges, but this made the going painfully slow; a typical entry in Wills' diary reads:[30]

Between four and five o'clock a heavy thunderstorm broke over us, having given very little warning of its approach....The rain was incessant and very heavy for an hour and a half, which made the ground so boggy that the animals could scarcely walk over it.

We nevertheless started at 10 minutes to 7am, and after floundering along for half an hour, halted for breakfast. We then moved on again, but soon found that the travelling was too heavy for the camels, so we camped for the remainder of the day....

He named some of their camps after the tribulations they faced: 'Humid Camp', 'Muddy Camp', 'Mosquito Camp'. Gray, who had been complaining of dysentery stole some of the flour from their precious packs, and was punished by Burke; he was thought to be shamming in order to escape some of his duties, but as it turned out he grew progressively weaker and died within only three weeks of the incident. The others scarcely had the strength to bury him.

A few days later they were elated to recognise their surroundings, and realised that they were nearing Cooper's Creek and their supply depot, but as they staggered into the old camp the shock-wave hit them that the place was deserted. There was no one there. Burke was totally overwhelmed and flung himself onto the ground in despair. On a tree were carved the words:

DIG
3 FT. N.W.
APR. 21 1861

They scrambled in the freshly turned dirt and found a box of provisions and a bottle containing the fateful message that Brahe and the rest of the depot had packed up and left that very day; after four months away, they had missed them by a matter of nine or ten hours.

Wills wrote:[31]

Sunday 21 April 1861. – Arrived at the depot this evening, just in time to find it deserted. A note left in the plant by Brahe communicates the pleasing information that they have started today for the Darling, their camels and horses all well and in good condition; we and our camels being just done up, and scarcely able to reach the depot have very little chance of overtaking them....our legs almost paralysed.....a trying task to walk only a few yards...

After a couple of days rest, Burke made the fatal decision that they should head west towards Adelaide, via Mount Hopeless, in theory a shorter route to settled districts, rather than follow in the wake of Brahe and Co down towards the Darling; both Wills and King preferred the latter course, but gave way to their leader.

The three men staggered off; they had provisions for about a month from the cache left for them, but the two surviving camels were almost done-in; within a few days they had shot one camel which got stuck in the mud, and cut off as much flesh as they could to eat; the other camel they had to abandon when it refused to get up. Some aborigines gave them some fish, but then disappeared into the desert.

On 27 May Wills returned alone to the depot at Cooper's Creek to see if by some remote chance any relief party had turned up; he arrived on 30 May. Incredible as it may seem, Brahe, on his way down to the Darling, had met Wright's party on their way up from Menindie and the two men had returned to Cooper's Creek on 9 May, just to make sure that nothing had happened in the interim – with fatal and almost criminal neglect they omitted to check the cache and so failed to realise that Burke had returned. Similarly Brahe and Wright failed to leave any obvious sign that they had been back to the depot and of course by the time Wills arrived, they had gone.

Wills re-opened the cache and buried his journal and letters, together with the following note:[32]

> Depot Camp, May 30th.
> We have been unable to leave the creek. Both camels are dead, and our provisions are exhausted. Mr Burke and King are down the lower part of the creek. I am about to return to them, when we shall probably come up this way. We are trying to live the best way we can, like the blacks, but find it hard work. Our clothes are going to pieces fast. Send provisions and clothes as soon as possible.
> W.J.Wills.
> The depot party having left contrary to instructions, has put us in this fix. I have deposited some of my journals here for fear of accident.
> W.J.W.

Wills then started out to rejoin Burke and King. He received friendly assistance from more aborigines on the way. The three companions together again survived on the wild plant 'nardoo', pounding the seeds to make little cakes – a technique they learnt from the aborigines – but although it satisfied their immediate hunger, it contained little nourishment; the three men were slowly starving to death. Wills' diary records their plight:[33]

> I feel much weaker than ever, and can scarcely crawl out of the mia-mia [a rough shelter of branches and twigs]. Unless relief comes in some form or other I cannot possibly last more than a fortnight. It is a great consolation at least, in this position of ours, to know that we have done all we could, and that our deaths will rather be the result of the mismanagement of others than of any rash act of our own. Had we come to grief elsewhere, we could only have blamed ourselves; but here we are returned to Cooper's Creek, where we had every reason to look for provisions and clothing, and yet have to die of starvation, in spite of the explicit instructions given by Mr Burke, that the depot party should await our return, and the strong recommendation by the Committee 'that we should be followed up by a party from Menindie'.

Wills was suffering from the cold, especially at night; his clothing consisted of a 'wide-awake' hat, a wool shirt, an over-shirt, the remains of a pair of flannel trousers, two pairs of socks in rags, and a waistcoat. Finding his weakness increasing, Wills pressed Burke and King to go in search of natives – the only hope of saving themselves. Wills gave Burke a letter and his watch for his father, then after an emotional farewell, they left him with a pile of nardoo cakes, some water and firewood.

On 29 June Wills made the last entry in his diary:[34]

> Friday, 29th June, 1861. – Clear, cold night; slight breeze from the east; day beautifully warm and pleasant. Mr.Burke suffers greatly from the cold, and is getting extremely weak. He and King start tomorrow up the creek to look for blacks; it is the only chance we have of being saved from starvation. I am weaker than ever, although I have a good appetite, and relish the nardoo much; but it seems to give us no nutriment, and the birds here are so shy as not to be got at. Even if we had a good supply of fish, I doubt whether we could do much work on them and the nardoo alone. Nothing now but the greatest good luck can save any of us; and as for myself I may live four or five days if the weather continues warm. My pulse is at forty-eight, and very weak, and my legs and arms are nearly skin and bone. I can only look out, like Mr Micawber, 'for something to turn up'. Starvation on nardoo is by no means very unpleasant, but for the weakness one feels, and the utter inability to move one's self....

Exhausted and undernourished, William Wills was left in a rough shelter while Burke and King went off in search of natives for help.

Only two days after leaving Wills, early in the morning, Burke died; King waited for a couple of days to try and regain his strength, then returned to where they had left Wills. He found him lying dead in his shelter.

It was not until 13 September that a relief expedition finally arrived at Cooper's Creek; the saga of delays, administrative bungles, procrastination and indecision is hard to believe. Alfred Howitt led the party and they quickly found King, living with the aborigines, but wasted to a shadow. When he had recovered sufficiently, he took the party to the place where Wills had died; they buried his remains and after a simple ceremony carved an inscription on a tree. Burke was likewise buried, and the party, together with King, returned to Melbourne.

Dr Wills later published his son's last letter:[35]

Cooper's Creek
Jun 27th 1861
My dear Father,
These are probably the last lines you will ever get from me. We are on the point of starvation, not so much from absolute want of food, but from want of nutriment in what we can get. Our position, although more provoking, is probably not near so disagreeable as that of poor Harry and his companions. We have had very good luck and made a most successful trip to Carpentaria and back to where we had every right to consider ourselves safe, having left a depot here, consisting of four men, twelve horses and six camels. They had sufficient provisions to have lasted them for twelve months with proper economy. We have also every right to expect that we should have been immediately followed up by another party with additional provisions and everything necessary for forming a permanent depot at Cooper's Creek. The party we had here had special instructions not to leave until our return, unless from absolute necessity. We left the creek with nominally three months' supply, but they were reckoned at little over the rate of half rations, and we calculated on having to eat some of the camels. By the greatest good luck at every turn we crossed to the Gulf through a good deal of fine country, almost in a straight line from here. On the other side the camels suffered considerably from wet, and we had to kill and jerk one soon after starting back. We had now been out a little more than two months, and found it necessary to reduce the rations considerably, and this began to tell on all hands, but I felt it by far less than either of the others. The great dryness and scarcity of game and our forced marching prevented us from supplying the defficiency from external sources to any great extent, and we never could have held out but for the crows and hawks and the portulac. The latter is an excellent vegetable and I believe secured our return to this place. We got back here in four months and four days and found that the others had left the creek the same day. We were not in a fit state to follow them. I find I must close this that it may be planted but I will write some more, although it has not so good a chance of reaching you as this. You will have great claims on the Committee

for their neglect. I leave you in sole charge of what is coming to me, the whole of my money I desire to leave to my sisters; other matters I will leave for the present.

Adieu, my dear Father. Love to Tom.　　　　　W.J.Wills
I think to live about four or five days. My religious views are not the least changed and I have not the least fear of their being so. My spirits are excellent.

When the full news of the disaster reached Melbourne there was uproar, and when King arrived the melée was so great that he took refuge in Government House. A Royal Commission of inquiry was ordered and Howitt was sent back to Cooper's Creek to disinter the bodies of Burke and Wills so that they could be accorded a proper public funeral with all the trappings. A letter, published in the *Express and Echo* not long after the centenary of these events, sums up what everyone felt: 'The expedition was the best equipped, the most expensive and the most incompetently conducted one in the history of Australian exploration'.[36]

The funeral was a tremendous affair; the bodies were carried in an elaborate hearse, a replica of that used at the Duke of Wellington's funeral in London ten years earlier, and drawn by six black horses. A huge monolith of undressed Harcourt stone was erected in the Melbourne cemetery and inscribed 'In memory of Robert O'Hara Burke and William John Wills....' and then a public fund was opened for a monument. The government contributed £4,000 and Charles Summers won the competition for its commission.

Back in Totnes, William Wills was not forgotten. The inhabitants, aided by contributions from Devonshiremen in Australia, erected a granite obelisk on the Plains, between the High Street and the bridge over the River Dart. The inscription reads:

In honour of
William John Wills
Native of Totnes
The First with Burke to cross the
Australian continent
He perished in returning, 28th June
1861.
Erected by Public Subscription
August 1864.

In the 1890s, a colonist from Devon, a Mr Angel, who returned from South Australia on a visit to Totnes and to his native parish of Littlehempston, found the inscription on the memorial was becoming obscure – he had it renewed on a tablet of white marble let into the granite; and later a medallion of Wills, by Mr F.Horn, a local marble mason, was fixed above the inscription.[37] This century, the centenary of Wills' death was marked by the commissioning of a plaque for the historic Guildhall in Totnes; the gift of the Government of Victoria, it was carved by Mark Batten and unveiled on 18 May 1962 by the Agent General for Victoria, Colonel Sir William Leggett.[38]

Medallion portrait of Wills

Dr Wills had his return passage to England paid by the Victorian Government; it also voted £2,090 to Mrs Wills, and £500 each to William's two sisters.[39] Back in Devon, the family moved to Ethelmead, Cleveland Road, Torquay, where Dr Wills re-established his medical practise.[40]

The Governor of Victoria, Sir Henry Barkly, in a letter to Mrs Wills, wrote:[41]

You may rely upon it that the name of William John Wills will go down to posterity, both at home and in this colony, amongst the

The Wills memorial obelisk on the Plains, Totnes (Devon)- Wills' home town.

The Burke and Wills monument, Melbourne, by Charles Summers; it was originally erected at the corner of Collins and Russell Streets in the heart of the city, but in 1886 it was moved to its present site outside Parliament House.

207

brightest of those who have sacrificed their lives for the advancement of scientific knowledge and the good of their fellow-creatures.

The same cannot be said for the vast majority of emigrants, who despite their pioneering spirit and undoubted bravery have slipped into obscurity, their stories and achievements forgotten and unrecorded. Only the isolated researches of family historians and genealogists occasionally throw up characters and events of such significance that they then filter into the history books. Otherwise most of the West Country men and women, united by their experience of facing that daunting voyage 13,000 miles around the world, are unknown; their names may feature on the sheaves of records in the National Archives, but their personal details and connections are untraced.

West Country people, particularly the rural poor, comprised a high proportion of emigrants to Australia; from successful merchant to convict, farm labourer to artist, all played their part in laying the foundations of that new society and in the creation of a new national character. The 'Australian' is an amalgam, and it is tempting to imagine that a significant part of the mixture has its roots in the English West Country.

'To know a country, you must know its memories'[42] and to know Australia you must therefore understand the origins of its settlers. Many, like old George Peppin, found it almost impossible to adjust to the upheaval, his roots in old England had gone too deep; but by the end of the nineteenth century, 'riding on the sheep's back', the sheep which he had so successfully adapted to the new conditions, Australia had the highest per capita income in the world and was well on the way to establishing its national identity free of colonial shackles.

The great blot on the history of Australia over the three centuries since William Dampier first strode ashore is the indifference, or worse, with which the aboriginals have been treated. The great Tasmanian race was wiped out within a couple of generations of the first European settlement in Tasmania; on the mainland the aboriginals survive, but too many live out a fringe existence neither enjoying the freedom of their traditional world nor participating in the imposed society of modern Australia. Whilst for them there is nothing to celebrate in 1988, for the rest let us hope that the future will bring greater understanding and a willingness to acknowledge the time-immemorial rights of the original inhabitants of the country.

NOTES TO THE TEXT

Chapter I
1 Blainey,G.*The Tyranny of Distance*,Sun Books,Melbourne, 1966.p.4.
2 Dampier,W.*A New Voyage*,Knapton,London,1697.
3 *idem*
4 Wilkinson,C.*William Dampier*,Bodley Head,London.1929.
5 Dampier,W.*op cit.*
6 *idem*
7 Dampier,W.*A Discourse on Winds, Tides and Currents*,London,1699.
8 Wilkinson,C.*op cit.*
9 *idem*
10 Dampier,W.*op cit.*
11 *Editorial notes to Dampier's Voyages*,ed.John Masefield.London, 1906,Vol 1.p350-1.
12 Wilkinson,C.*op cit.*
13 Evelyn,J.*The Diary of John Evelyn*,1698,ed.William Bray, 1818.p721.
14 Dampier,W.*A Voyage to New Holland*,Part I.Knapton,London,1703.
15 *Courts-Martial*,Official Minutes,P.R.O.
16 *London Gazette*No.3906

Chapter II
1 Blainey,G.*The Tyranny of Distance*,Melbourne,1966,p.9.
2 Wood,G.A.*The Discovery of Australia*,Macmillan,London,1922.p.369.
3 Cook,Capt.J.*Journals*,Vol I,p.399.
4 Stephens,S.E.&Cilento,Sir R.*Introduction to Cooktown and District*, 1976,p.3.
5 Hughes,R.*The Fatal Shore*,1987.
6 Whitlock,R.*Wiltshire*,Batsford.1976.p.133.
7 *Cook's Journal*,18 May 1773,quoted in Clark, C.M.H.*A History of Australia*,M.U.P.1963 ed.p.54.
8 Julen,H.*Brief Guide to the Discovery of Tasmania*,Launceston.p.2.
9 *ibid*.p.2.
10 *West Briton*,17 April 1840.
11 Journals of the House of Commons,Vol.XXXVII.
12 Journals of the House of Commons,Vol.XL,p.955.
13 Evidence of John Howard to Committee on the Hulks. Abstract from Journal of the House of Commons,15.4.1778.
14 Report of Select Committee on Secondary punishments, Parliamentary Papers 1831-2,VII,547.
15 Somerset County Record Office D/P/Cur.r.13/3/2.39c.
16 Somerset County Record Office D/P/Con.13/B/2.
17 Journals of the House of Commons,Vol.XL,p.1161.Lord Beauchamp's Report from Committee inquiring into Transportation Act of 1784.
18 Quoted in Robert Hughes,*The Fatal Shore*,from D.Mackay, *Place of Exile*,p.21.
19 Historical Records of New South Wales,Vol.1,Pt 2,p.14.18 August,1786.
20 See *The Tyranny of Distance* by Geoffrey Blainey,p.21-6; *The Fatal Shore* by Robert Hughes.
21 Historical Records of New South Wales,Vol.I,Pt 2,p.24.

AUSTRALIA BOUND

Chapter III

1 Quoted as frontispiece by T.S.Hughes,*Arthur Phillip*, Movement Publications,Cabarita.1982.

2 King,J.*The First Fleet*,London.1982.p.5.

3 *ibid*.p.27.

4 Hughes,R.*The Fatal Shore*,1985.King,J.*op cit*.p.29-30.

6 Various sources including John Cobley,*Crimes of the First Fleet Convicts*,in *The Sun Herald*.March 1970; Frank Clune, *The First Fleet at Norfolk Island*,First Fleeters,Vol.I,No.I, 1969; J.King,*The First Fleet*,1982.

7 Letter from Newton Fowell to his father, acquired by the City of Portsmouth in 1974. From a transcript per John Vivian.

8 Hughes,T.S.*Arthur Phillip*,*op cit*.p.24.

9 King,J.*op cit*.p.43.

10 *ibid*.p.55.

11 Fowell,N. quoted in *The Sydney Morning Herald*,25.7.87

12 Smyth,A.B. surgeon on Lady Penrhyn, quoted by J.King,*op cit*.p.75.

13 Collins,D. Judge Advocate on the *Sirius*,quoted by J.King, *op cit*.p.86.

14 Clark,R. quoted by J.King,*op cit*.p.89.

15 *idem*.p.95.

16 Phillip,A. quoted by J.King,*op cit*.p.102.

17 King,J.*op cit*.p.121.

18 Clark,R. quoted by J.King,*op cit*.p.151.

19 Clark,R. quoted by Robert Hughes in *The Fatal Shore*.

20 Phillip to Sydney, 15 May 1788,Historical Records of New South Wales, Vol I,Pt 2,pp.121-2

21 King,P.G. quoted by J.King,*op cit*.p.166.

22 Clark,R. quoted by J.King,*op cit*.p.169.

23 Quoted by J.King,*op cit*.pp.171-2; from Historical Records of New South Wales,Vol II.

24 From manuscript notes about the Small family supplied by John Vivian.

25 Clune,F.*The First Fleet at Norfolk Island*,First Fleeters, Vol I,No I,1969.

26 Tench,W.*A Complete Account of the Settlement at Port Jackson*, in New South Wales,London,1793,pp.80-1.

27 Phillip,A. to Lord Sydney quoted in T.S.Hughes *Arthur Phillip*. pp.61-62.

28 Payton,P.J.*The Cornish Miner in Australia*,1984.

29 Fowell,N. quoted in *The Sydney Morning Herald*,25.7.87.

30 Hughes,T.S.*Arthur Phillip*,p.82.

31 Fowell,N. quoted in *The Sydney Morning Herald*,25.7.87

32 *Australian Dictionary of National Biography*

33 Phillip,A. to W.Grenville,17.7.1790, Historical Records of Australia 1,pp.194-197.

34 Hughes,R.*op cit*.p.105.

35 Ede,M.*They Came to Bath*.Magazine article, source unknown.

36 Vivian,J. Letter to T.S.Hughes, January 1986, quoted by T.S.Hughes in *Arthur Phillip*.

37 This memorial was originally dedicated to Arthur Phillip in 1931 in St Mildred's Church, Bread Street, London, close to his place of birth. That church was destroyed by enemy bombing during the Second World War, but the bronze bust and panels were found and re-erected on a nearby new building at Gateway House in 1968. Subsequently, owing to vandalism, the bust and panel were copied and replicas re-erected, the originals being transferred to the care of the Phillip Memorial Trust.

38 Hughes,T.S.*op cit*,Addendum,p.109.

39 Joy,W.*The Exiles*,1973,p.197-8.

Chapter IV

1 From a manuscript scrapbook compiled by M.J.Conlon, in National Library, Canberra. Quoted in this form in *The Australian Legend* by Russel Ward, O.U.P.1978 ed.

2 *General Register*, Ilchester Gaol. Somerset County Record Office Q/AGi 14/1

3 Hudson,W.H.*A Shepherd's Life*,1910;1981 edition.

4 Inscription on the stone at Gore Cross; the Chitterne Down stone reads:
This monument is erected to record the awful end of Benjamin Colclough, Highway Robber, who fell Dead on this Spot in attempting to escape his pursuers after Robbing Mr Dean of Imber in the evening of Oct 21st, 1839, and was buried at Chitterne without funeral Rites.
The Robbery of the wicked shall destroy them.
Prov.21.7.
His three companions in Iniquity Thomas Saunders, George Waters, & Richard Harris were captured & sentenced at the ensuing Quarter Sessions at Devizes to Transportation for the Term of Fifteen Years.
Though hand join in hand the wicked shall not be unpunished.
Prov.11.21.

5 *Devizes and Wiltshire Gazette*, August 1840.

6 Kirkaldy,J.*Three Wiltshire Highwaymen in Australia*, Wiltshire Archaeological and Natural History Society Annual Bulletin, No.26, Spring 1980.p.3.

7 *idem*.p.4.

8 Billett,M.C.*Somerset Standard*,16.5.1986; and family papers kindly lent to the author.

9 Western,W.G.*John Western of Exeter and Sydney*, The Devon Historian,Vol.32,April 1986.

10 Clarke,M.*His Natural Life*,1870.Penguin ed.1970.

11 Snetzler,M.F.*Indicted – Transported – Innocent*, Devon Family Historian, No.32, October 1984,pp.19-20.

12 On A31 5 miles west of Wimborne. Map ref: SY8999 8840/9710.

13 Osborn,G.*Dorset Curiosities*.Dovecote Press,1986.pp.74-75.

14 *General Register*,Ilchester Gaol,1808-22.SCRO. Q/AGi 14/1

15 Specifications of a carriage to transport prisoners.SCRO Q/AG(w) 4/1

16 Escape of Prisoners.SCRO Q/AGi 16/4

17 Snetzler,M.F.*op cit*.p.19-20.

18 Quoted by Robert Hughes in *The Fatal Shore*,*op cit*.

19 *ibid*.

20 Report of the Select Committee on Transportation,pp.10-11,Parliamentary Papers,1812,II,341.

21 *ibid*.

22 Letter to E.F.Bromley; Parliamentary Papers,1819,VII,575.

23 Cunningham,P.*Two years in New South Wales*,Vol.II,1825.pp.212-4

24 Evidence of W.R.H.Brown to Select Committee on State of Gaols,p.99. Parliamentary Papers,1819,VII,575.

25 Bigge,J.T.*Report on the State of New South Wales*,p.61,1820.

26 *Report of Select Committee on Transportation*,p.11, Parliamentary Papers,1812,II,341.

27 King,P.G. to Nepean, 9 May 1803, Historical Records of Australia,I,4,p.248.

28 Hughes,R.*op cit*.

29 Clarke,M.*His Natural Life*,first published 1870,Penguin edition 1970,pp.463-465.

30 *Australian Dictionary of National Biography*.

31 *ibid*.

32 Denholm,D.A.*Let's Talk About Port Arthur*,4th edition,Tasmanian Tourist Council,1973.

33 Davies,D.M.*The Last of the Tasmanians*,1973.See Chapter 8, pp.157-182.

34 Exhibition catalogue,*Our Origins*,Council of the Library of New South Wales,1973.p.40.

35 Report of Select Committee on Transportation,p.xvii,Parliamentary Papers,1837-8,XXII,669.

36 Whately,R.*Transportation*.Miscellaneous Lectures and Reviews, 1833.pp.258-9.
37 Private letter from Lord John Russell to Sir William St Aubyn, 5 April 1837; St Aubyn family archives, Pencarrow, Cornwall. (By kind permission of Lady St Aubyn).
38 Report of the Select Committee on Transportation,p.xxxiii,Parliamentary Papers,1837-8,XXII,669.
39 St Aubyn, Sir William, speech to the House of Commons,6 March 1838.
40 Butler,J.M.*Convict by Choice*,Melbourne,1974.
41 Butler,J.M.*Settler by Succession*,Belmont,Victoria,1979.
42 Advertisment,Plymouth City Museum,Accession No.AR.1986.674.
43 Radcliffe,W.*Port Arthur Guide*,Port Arthur,undated,pp.35-37.
44 *Church Guide*,St Mary the Virgin,Wylye,p.2. and Sir Richard Colt Hoare,*History of Wiltshire*,1825.

Chapter V
Convict Tales:

Petty crooks:

1 Quarter Session Papers,Devon PRO,Epiphany,1828.
2 *Exeter Flying Post*,4.8.1828.
3 Thomas,N.*Branching Out*,Naracoote,South Australia,1981.p.4.
4 Convict Record of William Stanbury, Archives Office, Tasmania.
5 Henderson,A.*Journal from the York*,microfiche,Mitchell Library, Sydney, quoted by Neil Thomas,*op cit*.p.14.
6 Thomas,N.*op cit*.p.15
7 *ibid*.p.15.
8 *ibid*.p.15.
9 *ibid*.p.15.
10 *ibid*.p.16.
11 Western,W.G.*John Western of Exeter and Sydney 1824-1893*,The Devon Historian,Vol 32,April 1986.
12 Arthur,Sir George, quoted in *The Chain Gang*,c1835,Report of the Select Committee on Transportation,p.xiv,Parliamentary Papers,1837-8. XXII, 669.
13 Western,W.G.*op cit*.
14 *ibid*.
15 *ibid*.

Greenway:

1 *The Australian Encyclopaedia*,1965.p.382.
2 Quoted in *Programme of Events*,Clifton Village Fayre,15.7.1978. p.24.
3 Pevsner,N.*North Somerset and Bristol*,1958,p.449.
4 These windows, Pevsner noted, were added in 1894 by E.Henry Edwards.
5 Ellis,M.H.*Francis Greenway his life and times*,2nd ed.1953 and Clifton Village Fayre Programme.p.26.
6 *Programme of Events*,*op cit*.p.28.
7 Joy,W.*The Exiles*,Sydney,1972.p.173.
8 Editorial,*Compass*,No.12,December 1973.
9 *The Australian Encyclopaedia*,1965.p.383
10 Joy,W.*op cit*.p.198
11 Ellis,M.H.*The Australian Encyclopaedia*,1965.p.383.
12 Quoted by Ellis,*op cit*.p.383

NOTES TO THE TEXT

Tolpuddle Martyrs:
1 Traditional folk song.
2 Marlow,J.*The Tolpuddle Martyrs*,London 1971;1985 edition,p.41.
3 Loveless,G.from *Tolpuddle, an historical account through the eyes of George Loveless*,T.U.C.London,1984.p.10.
4 *idem*.p.12.
5 *idem*.p.16.
6 *Assize Calendar*,Dorchester,1834.
7 *Dorset County Chronicle*,20 March 1834.
8 Loveless,G.*op cit*.p.24.
9 *The Times*,21 March 1834.
10 Loveless,G.letter to his wife read in the House of Commons by Thomas Wakley,Hansard,25 June 1835.
11 *Pioneer*,29 March 1834.
12 Quoted by Joyce Marlow,*op cit*.p.128.
13 Marlow,J.*op cit*.p.156.
14 *idem*.p.165.
15 *idem*.p.166.
16 *idem*.p.169.
17 Hansard,14 March 1836.
18 Loveless,G.,*The Tasmanian*,30 September 1836.
19 *The Plymouth, Devonport and Stonehouse Herald*,24 March 1838.
20 *Plymouth and Devonport Weekly Journal*,19 April 1838.
21 *The Morning Chronicle*,17 April 1838.
22 Marlow,J.*op cit*.p.253.

Chapter VI
1 *Victoria County History*,Wiltshire,Vol IX,pp.320ff.
2 Cobbett,W.*Rural Rides*,1830. Penguin edition 1973.p.309.
3 *ibid*.p.304
4 *ibid*.p.320
5 *ibid*.p.332
6 *ibid*.p.340
7 Eden Sir F.M.*The State of the Poor*,1797, quoted by J.H.Bettey in *Dorset*,1974.p.217.
8 Quoted by J.H.Bettey in *Wessex from AD1000*,1986.
9 Heeley,A. and Brown,M.C.*Victorian Somerset – John Hodges a farm labourer*,Glastonbury,1978.pp.11-13.
10 Anon.c1840,Somerset Rural Life Museum Research papers.
11 Jefferies,R.*Hodge and His Masters*,1880.1979 ed.
12 Syvret,M. and Stevens,J.*Balleine's History of Jersey*,1981. p.238.
13 Report by Her Majesty's Commissioner and local clergy on conditions on the Somerset Levels, c1870, quoted by C.W.Green,*Victorian Somerset: Cottages*.Part II,1979,p.45.
14 Report of the Royal Commission on the Housing of the Working Classes, 1884.
15 Boyle,R.F.*Report on Somersetshire*,1869.
16 Bettey.J.H.*Dorset*,1974.
17 Jefferies,R.*Hodge and His Masters*,1880,p.291.
18 Anon.1856, quoted by T.Coleman,*Passage to America*,1972. Penguin ed.1976.p.41.
19 Garrett,R.*The Search for Prosperity*,London,1973,p.125.
20 Dickens,C.*The Personal History and Experience of David Copperfield the Younger*,London,1872.
21 Shaw,A.G.L.*The Story of Australia*,London,1955,5th edition,1983, p.74ff.

22 Braim,T.H.*New Homes: the rise, progress, present position and future prospects of the Australian Colonies and New Zealand*,London,1870. N.B.Thomas Braim, late Archdeacon of the Diocese of Melbourne, returned to England where he became Rector of Bishop's Caundle, near Sherborne, Dorset.

23 *Melbourne Argus*,quoted in T.H. Braim,*idem.*

24 *Devizes Gazette*,14 February 1850,quoted by M.Baker, in *Aspects of the Life of the Wiltshire Labourer,c1850*. Wiltshire Archaeological Magazine,74/75,1981 p.162.

25 *Devizes Gazette*,22 July 1852,*idem.*

26 *Melbourne Argus*,quoted in T.H.Braim,*op cit.*

27 Braim,T.H.*op cit.*

28 Bird,Dr quoted by T.H.Braim,*op cit.*

29 Brayshay,M.*Government Assisted Emigration from Plymouth in the 19th century*,Transactions of the Devonshire Association, Vol.11 p.185-213.

30 *idem.*

31 Moss,O.P.Devon Family Historian, No.37,January 1986.p.5.

32 PRO.CO.384/79 fo.456. Colonisation Circular No.7 March 1847.

33 Brayshay,M.*op cit.*

34 White,W.*Directory of Devonshire*,1850.

35 *idem.*

36 Billing,M.*Directory of Devonshire*,Birmingham,1857.p.665.

37 *idem.*p.666.

38 Baker,M.*Some Early Wiltshire Emigrants to Australia*,The Hatcher Review,Vol.2,No.17,1984.p.330

39 *idem.*p.330.

40 Jenkyns,Mrs J. letter,22 June 1987.

41 *The Plymouth, Devonport and Stonehouse Herald*,Saturday 17 March 1849.

42 Wiltshire Record Office,665/22,pp.113-117.Collingbourne Ducis Parish Journal.

43 *idem.*

44 *idem.*

45 Hull,A.*A Chronological Journal or diary of Wind, Weather & Observations on Agriculture and the Times and other curiosities and remarkable events kept at Walscombe, near Chard.* Somerset County Record Office, DD/CHG 36.

46 Queensland State Archives,Z599 (A2-45 IMM/111),transcribed and supplied to the author by Mrs Carolyn Randle.

47 Baker,J. quoted by Mark Baker,*op cit*,1984.

Chapter VII

1 Quoted by T.Braim,*op cit*,1870.

2 Charlwood,D.*The Long Farewell*,Penguin Books,1981.

3 Greenhill,B. quoted by D.Charlwood,*op cit.*

4 Charlwood,D.*op cit.*

5 Stamp,T.and C.*William Scoresby*,Whitby,1975.

6 Charlwood,D.*op cit.* and Scoresby,W.*Variation of the Compass in Iron Ships*,The Times,24 September 1854.

7 *The Plymouth, Devonport and Stonehouse Herald*,10 February 1849.

8 From a collection of Tabart family papers kindly supplied by Jane Evans, Weston-super-Mare.

9 *Dictionary of Medical and Surgical Knowledge and Complete Practical Guide in Health and Disease for families, Emigrants and Colonists*, Houlston and Son, London, 1850.

10 *idem.*

11 *idem.*

12 Grant,A.*Sailing Ships and Emigrants in Victorian Times*,Then and There Series,Longman,1972.
13 Blainey,G.*The Tyranny of Distance*,Melbourne.p.158.
14 *Dictionary of Medical and Surgical Knowledge*,*op cit.*
15 *idem*.
16 Prout,J.S.*Journal of a voyage from Plymouth to Sydney on board the Royal Sovereign*,London,1844.
17 Boase,F.*Modern English Biography*,1965.
18 Blake,S.*George Rowe, Artist and Lithographer*, Exhibition Catalogue,Cheltenham Art Gallery,1982. p.25.
19 Joseland,J.*Journal* kept on voyage from Portsmouth in the *Salsette*,1853, from a typescript in Woodspring Museum, Weston-super-Mare; the original was presented to the National Maritime Museum in 1977.
20 Anonymous account of a voyage to Port Phillip from Plymouth, January to May,1853,National Maritime Museum, Greenwich, manuscript, JOD/79.
21 Joseland,J.*op cit.*
22 Information from the caption of a model of the Mystery displayed in the Cornwall County Museum, Royal Institution of Cornwall, Truro, 1987.
23 Payton,P.J.*The Cornish Miner in Australia*,1984,p.119.
24 Caption to an illustration of the wreck from a painting by C.White; Weymouth Museum, 32/32.
25 Burnett,D.*Dorset Shipwrecks*,Dovecote Press,1982,p.11.
26 Caption to an illustration in Weymouth Museum, 35/31.
27 Goodridge,C.M.*Narrative of a voyage to the South Seas and the Shipwreck of the Princess of Wales*,Exeter,1838.
28 Blainey,G.*op cit.*pp.207-208.
29 Ball,A. and Wright,D.*S.S.Great Britain*,Newton Abbot,1981.
30 Blainey,G.*op cit.*p.208.
31 Braim,T.1870,*op cit.*
32 Ball,A. and Wright,D.*op cit.*
33 *idem*.

Chapter VIII
1 *Australian Dictionary of Biography*,pp.144-146 and 153-159.
2 Joy,W.*The Exiles,op cit*,p.60-62.
3 *Australian Dictionary of Biography*,p.145.
4 Robertson,E.G.*Early Buildings of Southern Tasmania*,Vol II,p.395 and 400.
5 Mackaness,G.ed.*Recollections of Life in Van Dieman's Land*,Sydney,May 1961.p.11-19.
6 *idem*.
7 Copies of these letters were kindly lent by Miss P.Cotton, West Bradley.
8 Austin,L.N. letter dated 3.7.1868.
9 Evans, J.*Woodspring Museum Hotline,Weston Mercury*,8.6.84.
10 Private communication from Mrs Brownjohn, Hampshire.
11 150th Anniversary Brochure, Royal Jersey Agricultural and Horticultural Society.1983.p.4.
12 Sharland,M.*Stones of a Century*,Hobart,1952.
13 Butler,J.M.*Convict by Choice*,Melbourne,1974.pp.76-77.
14 Clune,F.*Search for the Golden Fleece*,1965,p.122.
15 *idem*.p.122.
16 Peppin,G.(junior),diary for 1859, Mitchell Library, quoted by Clune,*op cit.*p.174.
17 *Argus*,Melbourne,13.7.1861,quoted by Clune,*op cit.*p.202.
18 *Pastoral Times*,16.8.1862, quoted by Clune,*op cit.*p.203.
19 *Pastoral Times*,April 1872, quoted by Clune,*op cit.*p.214.

22 From family papers kindly supplied by Mrs Elaine Thomson, Pomona, Queensland.

23 From manuscript of the Magisterial Enquiry held on 5 May 1866, Warwick.

24 Pryor,O.*Australia's Little Cornwall*,1963.

25 *West Briton*,8.5.1840.

26 Pryor,*op cit.*

27 Payton,P.J.*The Cornish Miner in Australia*,1984.

28 *idem* and Pryor *op cit.*

29 Payton,P.J.*op cit.*

30 Pryor,*op cit.*

31 Butler,J.M.*Convict by Choice*,Melbourne,1974.p.109.

32 *idem*.p.110.

33 *idem*.p.131.

34 *Langport and Somerton Herald*,26.5.1928.

35 Morland,J.C.Chairman of the Rural Industries Committee of the Somerset Rural Community Council, speech reported in the *Langport and Somerton Herald*,26.5.1928.

36 Evans,J.*Charles Summers*,exhibition catalogue, Woodspring Museum,1978.p.2.

37 *idem*.p.2.

38 Thomas,M.*A hero of the workshop and a Somersetshire Worthy, Charles Summers*,Weston-super-Mare,undated.p.17

39 *Australian Dictionary of Biography*,p.220.

40 *Australian Dictionary of Biography*,p.220; and *The Art Journal*,1872.p.69-72.

41 Evans,J.*op cit*.p.3.

42 *Australian Dictionary of Biography*.p.220.

43 Family papers kindly lent by Miss Q.Dyer, Teignmouth (Devon).

44 *Queensland Country Life*,14 April 1966.

45 *idem.*

Chapter IX

1 Quoted in *The Australian Legend*,by Russel Ward,O.U.P.1978 edition.

2 Ritchie,J.*Australia as we once were*,1973.p.85.

3 Ward,R.*The Australian Legend*,O.U.P.1978.p.138.

4 Garrett,R.*The Search for Prosperity*,London,1973,p.55.

5 Dunkerley,C.*The Cornish in Australia*,Cornish Scene,August, 1986,p.49.

6 Braim,T.*op cit.*

7 *North Devon Journal*,4.9.1851.

8 Grant,A.*Sailing Ships and Emigrants in Victorian Times*,Then and There Series,Longman,1972.

9 *North Devon Journal*,26.6.1852.

10 Grant,A.*op cit.*

11 *idem.*

12 Quoted in *The Australian Legend*,by Russel Ward,*op cit.*

13 La Trobe,C.J. Governor of Victoria, October 1852, quoted by J.Kitson, *Great Emigrations*,London,1972.p.90-91.

14 From family information kindly supplied by Mrs F.Mapstone, Glastonbury,1986.

15 *Channel Islands Family History Journal*,Nos.27,p.269 and 28,p.302,1985.

16 Grant,A.*op cit*.p.67.

17 *idem*.p.67.

18 Payton,P.J.*The Cornish Miner in Australia*,1984,p.118.

19 *idem.*

20 Butler,M.*Convict by Choice*,Melbourne,1974.p.86-87.

21 Clarke,M.*op cit*.p.706.

22 Blake,S.*George Rowe, Artist and Lithographer,*exhibition catalogue, Cheltenham Art Gallery and Museums,1982.pp.8-9.

23 *idem.*pp22-23.

24 *idem.*p23.

25 Rowe,G. letter to his wife written in London, 1852; copy supplied by courtesy of Dr C.W.Marshall and John Somers Cocks.

26 Blake,S.*op cit.*p.24.

27 *idem.*p.25.

28 *idem.*p.26.

29 *idem.*p.26.

30 Rowe,G. letter to his wife 23.7.1853, copies supplied by courtesy of Dr C. W.Marshall and John Somers Cocks.

31 *idem.*

32 Letters published in *La Trobe Library Journal,*Vol 3,No.12, October 1973.pp.90-96.

33 Blake,S.*op cit.*p.30.

34 *Melbourne Argus,*May 1857, quoted by Blake,*op cit.*p.30.

35 *La Trobe Library Journal,*Vol 3,No.12,October 1973,p.90.

36 Keneally,T.*et al.Australia: beyond the dreamtime,*BBC,1987. and *Western Daily Press,*31.7.87,*Aussies steal a march on West.*

37 Braim,T.*op cit.*

38 Ingleton,G.ed.*True Patriots All,*Sydney,1952,p.258.

Chapter X

1 Plymouth Marketing Bureau handout, May 1986.

2 *Major Edmund Lockyer*, published by Government of Western Australia,1984.

3 *idem.*

4 Lockyer,E.*Journal,*quoted in Gov.of W.Australia publication,*op cit.*

5 Caption to a portrait of Sir Richard Spencer, Lyme Regis Museum, Dorset.

6 *Australian Dictionary of Biography,*1788-1850,p.465.

7 *Australian Dictionary of Biography,*1788-1850,Vol.II,p.495.

8 idem.

9 Atkinson,C.T.*op cit,*p.251.

10 *Australian Dictionary of Biography,op cit.*

11 *idem.*

12 *idem.*

13 Atkinson,C.T.*The Dorsetshire Regiment,*Vol.I,1947,p.250.

14 Dorset Military Museum,The Keep,Dorchester.

15 Dutton,G.*Australia's Last Explorer, Ernest Giles,*1970.p.21.

16 *idem.*

17 Windeatt,T.W.*Wills – the Australian Explorer,*Transactions of the Devonshire Association,Vol 25,1893.p.390.

18 *idem.*p.391.

19 *idem.*p.391.

20 Moorehead,A.*Cooper's Creek,*1963.1977 ed.p.23.

21 *idem.*p.23.

22 *idem.*p.29.

23 Windeatt,T.W.op cit.p.393.

24 Wills,W. letter to a friend, quoted in *Cooper's Creek* by Alan Moorehead.p.40.

25 Wills,W. letter to a sister quoted by T.W.Windeatt,*op cit.*p.394.

26 Cartoon, *the Great Australian Exploration Race, The Melbourne Punch,* 1860.

27 Moorehead,A.*op cit*.p.58.
28 Wills,W.*Journal* quoted by Alan Moorehead,*op cit*.p.62.
29 Burke,R.O'H.*Journal* quoted by Alan Moorehead,*op cit*.p.67.
30 Wills,W.*op cit*.p.75.
31 *idem*.p.83.
32 Wills,W. quoted by T.W.Windeatt,*op cit*.p.400.
33 Wills,W.*Diary*,21 June 1861, quoted by T.W.Windeatt,*op cit*.p.400
34 Wills,W.*Diary*,29 June 1861. p.401.
35 Wills,W. letter to his father,27 June 1861, quoted by Moorehead,*op cit*. p.120-121.
36 Hosford,M.B.*Express and Echo*,30 August 1962.
37 Wideatt,T.W.*op cit*.p.405.
38 West Country Studies Library, Exeter, cuttings file.
39 Moorehead,A.*op cit*.p.161.
40 Burnett-Morris,R.Devon Notes and Queries,Vol 14,p.333.
41 Barkly,Sir H.letter to Mrs Wills, quoted by T.W.Windeatt,*op cit*.p.404.
42 Adam-Smith,P.*et al*.*Australia, beyond the dreamtime*,BBC,1987.

INDEX

*More books from **Ex Libris Press** are described below:*

Bath/Land's End
WEST COUNTRY TOUR: *Being the Diary of a Tour through the Counties of Somerset, Devon and Cornwall in 1797*
John Skinner   96 pages   £2.95

London/Land's End
GREEN ROAD TO LAND'S END: *Diary of a Journey on Foot from London to Land's End*
Roger Jones   144 Pages   £2.95

South Devon
TALL SHIPS IN TORBAY: *A Brief Maritime History of Torquay, Paignton and Brixham*
John Pike   144 pages   £3.95
IRON HORSE TO THE SEA: *Railways in South Devon*
John Pike   160 pages   £3.95
BETWIXT MOOR AND SEA: *Rambles in South Devon*
Roger Jones   96 pages   £2.95

Somerset
MENDIP RAMBLES: *12 Walks around the Mendip Hills*
Peter Wright   96 pages   £2.95
COLLIERS WAY: *History and Walks in the Somerset Coalfield*
Peter Collier   160 pages   £4.95

Wiltshire
CURIOUS WILTSHIRE
Mary Delorme   160 pages   £4.95
TOURING GUIDE TO WILTSHIRE VILLAGES
Margaret Wilson   160 pages   £3.95

Farming Autobiography
SEEDTIME TO HARVEST: *A Farmer's Life*
Arthur Court   128 pages   £3.95

Ghost Stories
OUR NEIGHBOURLY GHOSTS: *Tall and Short Stories from the West Country*
Doreen Evelyn   96 pages   £2.95

The above books may be obtained through your local bookshop or from the publisher, post-free, at *1 The Shambles, Bradford on Avon, Wiltshire; Tel 02216-3595.* A full explanatory list will be sent upon request.